ENTERTAINING
WITH
FRIENDS

ENTERTAINING
WITH
FRIENDS

Jeni Wright *I*nspirational ideas for harmonising food, mood and friends

❦ Foreword by Glynn Christian ❦

Published with the assistance of The Southern Comfort Company

Ebury Press
LONDON

Published by Ebury Press
Division of the National Magazine Company Limited
Colquhoun House
27–37 Broadwick Street
London W1V 1FR

First impression 1987

ISBN 0 85223 646 8

Edited by Veronica Sperling
Art Direction by Frank Phillips
Designed by Peter Laws
Photography by Jan Baldwin
Styling by Cathy Sinker
Cookery by Maxine Clark

All photography by Jan Baldwin except for the following:
Coeurs à la Crème; Two-Tier Gooey Chocolate Cake; Barbecued
Bananas; Strawberry and Orange Mousse; Lamb Cutlets in Pastry;
Gazpacho; Aubergine Caviar by Paul Kemp,
and Frudités by James Jackson.

Computerset in Great Britain by MFK Typesetting Ltd, Hitchin, Herts.
Printed and bound in Italy by New Interlitho, S.p.a., Milan.

CONTENTS

*P*riorities. That's what Jeni Wright has bothered about, and that is why she has written such a worthwhile book. You see, successful entertaining at home has nothing to do with an avalanche of courses, or garnishes which take longer to prepare than the dishes. Entertaining is enjoying the company of friends, and sharing a meal with them is the oldest and most sincere form of hospitality. Naturally, providing the best you can, and presenting it as attractively as possible is part of the pleasure. But it is your guests who must be the stars of the evening, not the food. If it is, you have gone over the top of the culinary mountain, or you have invited the wrong people. Or both.

In *Entertaining With Friends* Jeni has this important balance, the priorities, just right. Mercifully free of fashionable posturing, it eschews the sudden clichés of scattered chives and no-fat fats and concentrates on the single worthwhile basic – good flavour honestly achieved. I much admire the way her fascinating menus turn out to be a well-planned balance of dishes which won't take forever to make. Neither must you trudge to Trincomalee for the ingredients. Thank goodness for food writers who know you can't taste time or effort, and who concentrate on food which is for eating rather than for admiring.

An original touch to some of Jeni's recipes is the addition of a dash of Southern Comfort – under-pinning existing flavours and creating new and exciting ones. Southern Comfort is the liquid embodiment of the hospitable traditions of America's south – a form of warm and genuine hospitality that special guests deserve to receive and which, with Jeni's help, you'll delight in giving.

Even the illustrations in *Entertaining With Friends* encourage me immediately to make lists of people I want to see at my table. You can see at a glance they are of real food planned to be made and enjoyed by home cooks who like giving pleasure to their friends. But most of all Jeni Wright's book offers you fun. And if you don't have fun entertaining you definitely do have your priorities in a muddle. Trust Jeni's menus to do it right.

Be assured, you'll make friends with this book, for it is the very paradigm for entertainers. I hope Jeni has my telephone number ...

SPRING

Spring is the time to shake off winter blues. The weather is improving every day and most of us feel in a more cheerful mood, glad to meet up with friends that perhaps we haven't seen for a while. From a romantic candlelit 'dinner à deux' to a Californian beach party, this chapter has plenty of entertaining ideas for you to choose from.

SPRING FEVER

SERVES 2

·

Hearts of Cheese

·

**Flambéed Duck Breasts
with Orange**

·

Passion Fruit Parfait

·

*W*hen spring is in the air, turn your partner's fancy with this romantically inspired menu for two. Create the frenzied feel of spring by filling every vase with flowers. Daffodils, narcissi and tulips are bright and sunny, while sweet-smelling freesias herald a heady springtime mood as they fill the air with their fresh perfume. For best effect at this time of year, position the dining table close to a window and entertain at lunchtime to let natural daylight enhance the look of the food. Sweep away the cobwebs and clutter of winter and keep the table as simple as possible. A plain cloth, cutlery and china give an instant uncluttered look, and show off the food to perfection. A hint of gold will reflect the rays of sunshine: plain and simple gold-plated cutlery looks sumptuous, but if you prefer a more subtle effect you can restrict the gold to a simple rim on the china. A cloth of shimmering moiré will also pick up the sumptuous effect of the gold to give a romantic mood, and if you serve Buck's Fizz or Suze with soda as an aperitif you will set the tastebuds tingling right from the start.

HEARTS OF CHEESE

Roll out the pastry on a lightly floured surface until 5 mm (¼ inch) thick. Cut out 2 hearts using a 7.5 cm (3 inch) heart-shaped pastry cutter. Press a 5 cm (2 inch) heart-shaped cutter in the centre of each heart, cutting about halfway through the thickness of the pastry. Roll out the pastry trimmings and cut two 5 cm (2 inch) hearts for the lids.

Place the shapes on a wetted baking sheet and chill in the refrigerator for about 30 minutes.

Meanwhile, make the filling: remove any rind from the chèvre. Mash the cheese in a bowl with the cream, herbs, cayenne and a pinch of salt.

Bake the pastry hearts at 220°C (425°F) mark 7 for 15–20 minutes until well risen and golden. Remove from the oven and carefully scoop out the centres of the large hearts. Spoon the filling into the centres. Brush the edges of the large hearts and the lids with beaten egg, then sprinkle with the walnuts. Return to the oven for 2–3 minutes until the cheese is just heated through and the pastry is glazed.

To serve: place the hearts on warm individual plates, arrange the lids on top and garnish with walnut halves and herbs.

Use ready-made puff pastry, available from the chilling cabinets of supermarkets and delicatessens. For the filling, try to select a good mixture of different fresh herbs – marjoram, chervil, chives, thyme, mint and parsley. Dried herbs simply will not do.

INGREDIENTS
100–150 g (4–5 oz) chilled puff pastry

a little beaten egg, to glaze

2 teaspoons finely chopped walnuts

FILLING
50–75 g (2–3 oz) chèvre (goat's cheese)

2 tablespoons single (light) cream

2 tablespoons chopped fresh herbs

¼ teaspoon cayenne pepper

salt

TO GARNISH
walnut halves

sprigs of fresh herbs

FLAMBEED DUCK BREASTS WITH ORANGE

Chilled duck breasts, often called suprêmes, can be found at large supermarkets. If not available, buy a whole duck; it is easy to remove the breast fillets from either side of the breastbone with a sharp knife. The remaining duck can be divided into portions and casseroled, or the meat can be used in a pâté or terrine, and the carcass to make a good stock.

INGREDIENTS
2 boneless duck breasts each weighing about 175 g (6 oz), skin and fat removed

freshly ground black pepper

1 tablespoon walnut or groundnut oil

15 g (½ oz/1 tablespoon) butter

2 tablespoons Southern Comfort

100 ml (3½ fl oz/scant ½ cup) duck or chicken stock

finely grated rind and juice of 1 large orange

2 teaspoons tomato purée

4 allspice berries, crushed

salt

a few orange segments, to garnish

Put the duck breasts between 2 sheets of greaseproof (waxed) paper and flatten slightly with a rolling pin. Sprinkle the breasts on both sides with pepper to taste. Heat the oil and butter in a heavy sauté pan, add the duck breasts and fry over moderate heat for 3–4 minutes on each side until the flesh changes colour.

Warm the Southern Comfort gently in a separate small pan. Remove the sauté pan from the heat. Ignite the Southern Comfort off the heat, then pour flaming over the duck breasts. Allow the flames to subside.

In a jug, mix together the stock, orange rind and juice, tomato purée, allspice and a pinch of salt. Return the sauté pan to the heat, pour over the sauce and simmer gently for 20 minutes until the duck feels tender when pierced with a skewer.

To serve: remove the duck from the sauce, slice thinly and keep hot on warm dinner plates. Strain the sauce and return to the rinsed-out pan. Boil rapidly to reduce by half, then taste for seasoning. Fan out each duck breast and pour the sauce over. Garnish with the orange segments.

PASSION FRUIT PARFAIT

This smooth, luscious ice cream is so good that you are bound to want more. It will keep for up to 2 months in the freezer, so why not make a double quantity and freeze half for another occasion? A measuring jug is used to whisk one egg white to obtain maximum volume.

INGREDIENTS

1 egg, separated

25 g (1 oz/2 tablespoons) caster (superfine) sugar

3 passion fruit

150 ml (¼ pint/⅔ cup) double (heavy) or whipping cream

Put the egg yolk and sugar in a heatproof bowl standing over a pan of gently simmering water. Whisk with a rotary or electric beater or a balloon whisk until thick and mousse-like. Stand the bowl in another bowl half filled with ice cubes and water and whisk until the mixture is cold.

Cut 2 of the passion fruit in half and scoop out the pulp. Whip the cream until it just holds its shape. Fold the pulp and cream into the mousse. Whisk the egg white in a measuring jug until stiff, then fold into the mousse. Pour into 2 long parfait or knickerbocker glory glasses, cover and freeze overnight.

To serve: remove the glasses from the freezer. Cut the remaining passion fruit in half and scoop out the flesh on top of the parfaits. Serve immediately.

C risp and crunchy mange-tout are
the perfect accompaniment to
beautifully tender and moist
*Flambéed Duck Breasts with Orange (page 9). This whole menu is simplicity
itself to prepare as so much can be made in advance. The Passion Fruit
Parfait (page 10) for dessert can be frozen as much as a week ahead of time.*

FLASH IN THE PAN

SERVES 4
·
Spaghetti alla Vongole
·
Chicken with Parma Ham and Cheese
·
Frudités
·

*I*f you are entertaining midweek with only a limited amount of time to prepare and cook before your guests arrive, informality is the keynote to success. This simple yet inspired menu allows you to entertain in informal style at lightning speed with minimum fuss.

A midweek supper party should unwind your guests no matter how frenetic a day they've had. With a little forethought and planning, it's easy to create a relaxed atmosphere within an hour or so of arriving home yourself. The secret lies in getting most of the preparation out of the way the night before and, luckily, most of this menu can be prepared in advance. But it's not only the food that counts. Leave everything ready before you go out in the morning – even the table can be set the night before and glasses put out for pre-dinner drinks. Once you're home, arrange nibbles around the room, draw the curtains, and set the music and the lighting low. Side lamps and spotlights provide a far more relaxing atmosphere than harsh centre lighting, and dimmer switches subdue the mood even more. Finish off any last-minute touches to the food, then allow yourself at least a little time to relax, before guests arrive.

SPAGHETTI ALLA VONGOLE

The clam sauce (salsa alla vongole) can be served with fresh pasta instead of the spaghetti suggested here. Choose a thin variety of noodles such as paglio e fieno, which is both green and white, and cook for just 3 minutes. Make the sauce the night before, then all you have to do just before the meal is quickly reheat it while the spaghetti or other pasta is cooking.

INGREDIENTS

15 g (½ oz/1 tablespoon) butter

2 tablespoons olive oil

1 medium onion, skinned and finely chopped

two 290 g (10½ oz) cans clams in brine, drained

1 garlic clove, skinned and crushed

4 tablespoons chopped fresh continental (flat-leaved) parsley

150 ml (¼ pint/⅔ cup) dry white wine

400 g (14 oz) can passata (sieved Italian tomatoes) or chopped tomatoes

salt

freshly ground black pepper

400 g (14 oz) spaghetti

freshly grated Parmesan cheese, to serve

Melt the butter with half of the oil in a heavy saucepan, add the onion and cook gently, stirring frequently, for about 5 minutes until soft but not coloured. Add the clams, garlic and half of the parsley, cook for a few minutes more, then add the wine and bring to the boil, stirring. Add the tomatoes and salt and pepper to taste, cover and cook gently for 15 mintues.

Meanwhile, bring a large saucepan of salted water to the boil, add the remaining oil, then the spaghetti and bring back to the boil. Simmer gently, uncovered, for 12 minutes or until al dente (tender but firm to the bite). Drain thoroughly.

To serve: pile the spaghetti in a warm serving dish. Stir the remaining parsley into the sauce, taste for seasoning and pour over the spaghetti. Hand Parmesan cheese separately.

CHICKEN WITH PARMA HAM AND CHEESE

Slice each chicken breast in half horizontally. Mix the flour on a sheet of greaseproof (waxed) paper with the herbs and pepper to taste and use to coat the chicken. Melt the butter with the oil in a heavy frying pan (skillet). Add as many pieces of chicken as the pan will hold in a single layer and fry for about 3 minutes on each side until golden and tender. Remove with a fish slice (pancake turner) and fry the remainder.

Arrange half of the chicken pieces in a lightly buttered ovenproof dish. Place the Parma ham on top and cover with the remaining chicken pieces. Sprinkle over the vermouth or wine, then cover completely with the grated cheese. Flash under the grill (broiler) for 5 minutes until the cheese is bubbling and golden. Serve straight from the dish.

Although Parma ham is available in packets from large supermarkets, the best quality is the kind you buy freshly sliced at Italian delicatessens. Ask for it by its Italian name of prosciutto.

INGREDIENTS

4 boneless chicken breasts, skinned
2 tablespoons plain (all-purpose) white flour
4 teaspoons chopped fresh basil
½ teaspoon dried mixed herbs
freshly ground black pepper
25 g (1 oz/¼ stick) butter
2 tablespoons olive oil
4 slices of Parma ham
6 tablespoons dry white vermouth or wine
175 g (6 oz/1½ cups) Fontina or Bel Paese cheese, grated

*N*othing is more tempting than this
colourful arrangement of Frudités
(page 16) – fresh seasonal fruits
served with a luscious creamy dip.

The earthenware pot opposite doubles up as both a cooking and serving dish for
Tagine (page 17), setting off the colours of the chicken and fruit perfectly.

FRUDITES

The fruits listed here are only a suggestion as you can use any fruit in season. Try to contrast soft and crisp textures and include at least one exotic variety such as star fruit, sharon fruit or kiwi.

INGREDIENTS

150 ml (¼ pint/⅔ cup) whipping cream
90 ml (6 tbsp) Greek strained yogurt
10 ml (2 tsp) clear honey
175 g (6 oz) fresh apricots
100 g (4 oz/1 cup) green grapes
100 g (4 oz/1 cup) black grapes
1 punnet (about 225 g/½ lb) fresh strawberries
2 crisp eating apples
2 bananas
juice of 1 lemon

Whip the cream, yogurt and honey together until the mixture just holds its shape. Pipe or spoon into 4 individual dishes.

Halve and stone (pit) the apricots. Halve the grapes (if not seedless) and flick out the seeds with the point of a knife. Wash the strawberries if necessary, but do not hull them. Quarter and core (do not peel) the apples, then slice thinly. Peel and slice the bananas. Immediately sprinkle both apples and bananas with lemon juice to prevent discoloration.

To serve: arrange the fruits on individual plates, with the individual cream dips on the side.

MOROCCAN MENU

SERVES 4
·
Tagine
·
Fresh Orange Frappé
·

Capture the mood of Morocco with this simple menu centred around a tagine of chicken and fruit. Tagine is the name for both the earthenware cooking pot in which a Moroccan stew is made and for the food itself. Traditional tagines are available for a reasonable price at specialist kitchenware shops, and it is well worth buying one if you are keen to give the meal authenticity.

In Morocco the table for eating is always low – usually a large brass tray on squat legs – and seating is either on cushions or mattresses on the floor. This is easy to copy at home using a low coffee table and cushions or pillows. Moroccan homes are richly decorated and draped with silk, velvet and embroidery; you can use lengths or remnants of velvet and silky material to cover your table and pillows. If you have any brass trays, jugs and pots these will also help your table to look Moroccan, as will earthenware plates and bowls and basketware. Aromatic, spicy or jasmine-scented incense sticks will instantly create a Middle Eastern atmosphere. A Moroccan gesture of hospitality is to lay out bowls of perfumed water for guests to rinse their fingers. Sweet mint tea offered as a digestif will round off the meal in true Moroccan style.

TAGINE

Cut each chicken portion into 2 pieces and strip off the skin. Melt the butter with the oil in a flameproof casserole, add the chicken portions in batches and fry over moderate heat until golden on all sides. Remove with a slotted spoon and place in the bottom of the tagine.

Add the onion to the casserole and fry gently for about 5 minutes until softened. Add the spices and fry for a further 2 minutes, stirring. Pour in the stock and bring to the boil. Add the fruit and salt and pepper to taste, then pour over the chicken. Cover tightly with the tagine lid. Cook at 150°C (300°F) mark 2 for 2 hours without lifting the lid.

To serve: carry the covered tagine to the table and very carefully lift the lid, taking care that the casserole juices do not spill out.

Tagines are earthenware and are therefore best not used over direct heat. For this reason the ingredients are first cooked in a flameproof casserole and then transferred to the tagine for cooking in the oven.

INGREDIENTS
4 chicken portions
50 g (2 oz/½ stick) butter
1 tablespoon olive oil
1 onion, skinned and sliced
2 teaspoons ground ginger
2 teaspoons paprika
2 teaspoons turmeric
½ teaspoon ground cinnamon
300 ml (½ pint/1¼ cups) chicken stock
225 g (½ lb) dried prunes and apricots
salt
freshly ground black pepper

FRESH ORANGE FRAPPE

Put the sugar in a heavy saucepan, add 300 ml (½ pint/ 1¼ cups) water and heat gently, stirring occasionally, until the sugar has dissolved. Increase the heat and boil rapidly for 2 minutes, without stirring. Leave until cold.

Stir the orange juice and orange flower water into the cold sugar syrup. Pour into a shallow freezer container and freeze for about 2 hours until slushy around the edges.

Turn the mixture into a bowl and beat with a fork to break up the ice crystals. Whisk the egg whites until they will hold soft peaks, then fold into the frappé. Return to the freezer for at least 4 hours until firm, preferably overnight.

To serve: break up the frappé with a fork, then spoon into individual glasses. Spoon 1 teaspoon Southern Comfort over each and serve immediately.

Southern Comfort is the perfect liqueur to spoon over this melt-in-the-mouth tangy ice. But be quick when you serve it or the frappé will melt.

INGREDIENTS
100 g (4 oz/½ cup) granulated sugar
150 ml (¼ pint/⅔ cup) freshly squeezed orange juice
1 teaspoon orange flower water
2 egg whites
4 teaspoons Southern Comfort, to serve

MAD HATTER'S TEA PARTY

SERVES 6–8
·
Pinwheel Sandwiches
Two-Tier
Gooey Chocolate Cake
·
Glazed Fruit Tartlets
·
Fruity Scones
·
Raspberry Trifle
·

*T*urn a tea party into a memorable occasion with these special teatime treats. Whether it's a cosy Sunday afternoon tea with the family or a more formal occasion such as a christening or birthday, this fabulous food fits the bill beautifully.

Teatime food deserves extra special loving care and attention, so take time for presenting your teatime food properly. Your pinwheel sandwiches must be the most delicate and dainty ever, the glazed fruit tarts the most perfectly presented and the glorious old-fashioned trifle prettily piped. Get out your 'Sunday best' china. Tea is definitely the occasion for it, and the prettier and more delicate it is the better – tea always tastes best drunk from a fine bone china cup. Crisp white damask cloths and napkins, trays and tray cloths can really come into their own at teatime, and if you have any lace or crochet, then this is the time to fetch it out for a traditional Victorian or Edwardian look. Doileys and cake stands, tea strainers and silver pastry forks can all add to the theme – with a pretty arrangement of flowers in the centre of the table. Roses, ranunculi and gypsophila in a cut-glass vase look particularly pretty in a teatime setting.

PINWHEEL SANDWICHES

Two small loaves make what seems to be an enormous number of pinwheels, but as they are dainty and bite-sized, most people can eat quite a few and there is no point in making less.
Very fresh bread is an absolute must for making pinwheels successfully. If the bread is not fresh, it will not roll without cracking.

INGREDIENTS	
105 g (4 oz) can red salmon	3–4 tablespoons finely chopped fresh watercress or parsley
175 g (6 oz/¾ cup) full-fat soft cheese (cream cheese)	½ teaspoon French mustard
	freshly ground black pepper
2–4 tablespoons thick mayonnaise	1 very fresh small white sandwich loaf
1 teaspoon lemon juice	
¼ teaspooon cayenne pepper	1 very fresh small wholemeal (whole wheat) sandwich loaf
salt	
2 hard-boiled (hard cooked) eggs, shelled and finely chopped	75–100 g (3–4 oz/¾–1 stick) butter, softened

Drain the salmon. Flake the flesh in a bowl, discarding the skin, then mash finely. Add half of the soft cheese, 1–2 tablespoons of the mayonnaise, the lemon juice, cayenne pepper and salt to taste. Beat with a wooden spoon until well combined.

Put the remaining cheese in a separate bowl with the chopped

*T*he jewel-bright colours of Glazed Fruit Tartlets (page 21) and the sweet temptation of Raspberry Trifle (page 22) are bound to appeal to your teatime guests. And Two-Tier Gooey Chocolate Cake (page 20), with its luscious double layers of chocolate mousse and cake, is a must for chocoholics.

eggs, 1–2 tablespoons mayonnaise, watercress or parsley, mustard and salt and pepper to taste. Beat with a wooden spoon until well combined.

Cut all the crusts off each loaf of bread except the base, to make a squared-off shape. Turn the loaf on its side and, holding the base, cut lengthways into 7 thick slices. Discard the base crust. Spread one side of each slice with butter.

Spread the white bread with the egg filling, the brown bread with the salmon. Roll up each slice from one short end then wrap individually in cling film (plastic wrap). Chill in the refrigerator for 2–4 hours until firm.

To serve: unwrap, cut each roll into 6 slices and arrange on a serving plate.

TWO-TIER GOOEY CHOCOLATE CAKE

The secret of melting chocolate successfully is not to let it get too hot. Always melt chocolate in a bowl over a pan of hot water, not directly in the pan itself, making sure that the bottom of the bowl does not touch the water.

BOTTOM LAYER

225 g (8 oz/1⅓ cups) plain (semi-sweet) dessert chocolate pieces

1 tablespoon Southern Comfort

5 eggs, separated

150 g (5 oz/¾ cup) caster (superfine) sugar

100 g (4 oz/1 stick) unsalted butter

Grease a 20 cm (8 inch) springform tin and line with grease-proof (waxed) paper. Grease the paper.

Make the bottom layer of the cake: place the chocolate in a heatproof bowl over a pan of gently simmering water. Heat gently until the chocolate melts, stirring once or twice. Stir the Southern Comfort into the chocolate and remove the bowl from the heat.

Put the egg yolks and sugar in a bowl and whisk with an electric beater until thick and creamy. Beat in the butter a little at a time until smooth. Beat in the melted chocolate until smooth.

In a separate clean bowl, whisk the egg whites until stiff, then fold into the chocolate mixture. Turn into the prepared tin. Bake at 180°C (350°F) mark 4 for 40 minutes until risen and firm. Leave the cake to cool in the tin for 1 hour.

Make the top layer of the cake: melt the chocolate and stir in the

Southern Comfort as for the bottom layer. Remove the bowl from the heat, cool for 1–2 minutes, then beat in the egg yolks. Whisk the egg whites until stiff as before and fold into the chocolate mixture.

Press the crust down on the baked cake with your fingers. Pour the top layer over the cake in the tin. Chill in the refrigerator overnight.

To serve: remove the cake carefully from the tin. Sprinkle grated chocolate around the edge and decorate with the shreds of orange zest.

TOP LAYER
225 g (8 oz/1⅓ cups) plain (semi-sweet) dessert chocolate pieces

2 tablespoons Southern Comfort

4 eggs, separated

TO DECORATE
grated chocolate

blanched needle shreds of orange zest

GLAZED FRUIT TARTLETS

Sift the flour and salt into a large bowl. Cut the butter into the flour in small pieces, then rub in lightly with the fingertips until the mixture resembles fine breadcrumbs. Stir in the sugar. Make a well in the centre and add the egg yolks and vanilla essence. Mix quickly with a knife, then gather together with the fingertips and knead very lightly to make a smooth ball of dough. Chill in the refrigerator for about 30 minutes.

Roll out the dough thinly on a lightly floured surface and use to line twelve 100 ml (3½ fl oz/½ cup) individual moulds. Prick with a skewer, then chill in the refrigerator for 15 minutes.

Line the dough with foil and fill with baking beans. Bake blind at 190°C (375°F) mark 5 for 15 minutes. Remove the foil and beans, then return to the oven for 3–5 minutes until the pastry is golden and crisp. Leave the pastry cases to cool in the moulds for a few minutes, before removing.

Melt the redcurrant jelly with the lemon juice. Brush over the inside of the pastry cases and immediately arrange the strawberries in the cases. Brush with the remaining glaze. Leave until set before serving.

You can use any shape of mould for these tartlets, as long as their capacity is roughly the same. Little boats (barquettes) look pretty, as do fluted individual quiche shapes, or even hearts. A mixture of different shapes looks good on one serving plate or tray. Different fruits can be used instead of the strawberries, or you can use a mixture of fruits such as halved grapes, whole raspberries, sliced peaches and kiwi.

INGREDIENTS
100 g (4 oz/1 cup) plain (all-purpose) white flour

pinch of salt

50 g (2 oz/½ stick) butter

50 g (2 oz/¼ cup) caster (superfine) sugar

2 egg yolks

few drops of vanilla essence (extract)

5 tablespoons redcurrant jelly

juice of ½ lemon

225 g (½ lb) strawberries, hulled and sliced

FRUITY SCONES

It is really worth using buttermilk to make scones as it gives a lighter, more digestible result. Look for buttermilk in the dairy section of supermarkets and in delicatessens, especially those specializing in Jewish food. Serve scones warm, with butter, jam and clotted or whipped cream.

INGREDIENTS

225 g (8 oz/2 cups) self-raising flour

1 teaspoon baking powder

½ teaspoon salt

50 g (2 oz/⅓ cup) sultanas (golden raisins), seedless raisins or chopped dates

40 g (1½ oz/3 tablespoons) butter

150 ml (¼ pint/⅔ cup) buttermilk

Sift the flour, baking powder and salt into a bowl. Stir in the fruit. Rub in the butter, make a well in the centre and add the buttermilk. Mix with a palette knife (metal spatula) to form a soft dough.

Turn the dough out on to a lightly floured surface and knead gently until free of cracks. Roll out until 2 cm (¾ inch) thick, then cut out 12 scones with a 5 cm (2 inch) fluted pastry cutter, re-rolling the trimmings as necessary. Leave to stand for 10–15 minutes.

Meanwhile, preheat a baking sheet in the oven at 230°C (450°F) mark 8. When ready to cook, place the scones on the heated baking sheet. Bake for 8–10 minutes until well risen and golden brown.

To serve: cool for a few minutes on a wire rack, then transfer to a cake plate or stand.

RASPBERRY TRIFLE

Don't skimp on the overnight soaking as this allows the flavour of the sherry to mellow into the cake.

INGREDIENTS

8 trifle sponges (small sponge cakes)

100 g (4 oz/⅓ cup) raspberry jam

150 ml (¼ pint/⅔ cup) sherry

600 ml (1 pint/2½ cups) milk

1 vanilla pod (bean), split

3 eggs

2½ tablespoons caster (superfine) sugar

2 teaspoons cornflour (cornstarch)

450–700 g (1–1½ lb) raspberries, defrosted if frozen

TO SERVE

300 ml (½ pint/1¼ cups) whipping cream

glacé (candied) cherries

angelica 'leaves'

Cut the trifle sponges horizontally in half, then sandwich back together with the jam. Place in the bottom of a glass bowl and spoon over the sherry. Set aside.

Pour the milk into a pan, add the vanilla pod and bring slowly to the boil. Cover with a lid, remove from the heat and leave to infuse for 20 minutes.

Beat the eggs, 2 tablespoons of the sugar and the cornflour in a bowl. Remove the vanilla pod from the milk, then stir a little milk into the egg mixture. Pour into the milk in the pan and simmer gently, stirring all the time with a wooden spoon until thick. Pour into a clean metal pan, sprinkle the surface with the remaining sugar and leave to cool.

Place the raspberries on top of the trifle sponges, then pour over the cold custard. Cover and leave overnight.

To serve: whip the cream until it holds its shape, then pipe or swirl over the custard. Decorate with cherries and angelica.

*A*rrange crisp raw vegetables and quails' eggs decoratively on platters for dunking into Piquant Tomato and Garlic Dip (page 24) and Devilled Crab Dip (page 25). Get your guests quickly in the party mood with Sparkling Celebration Cup (page 27).

DIPS, DUNKS AND DRINKS

SERVES 20–25

·

**Piquant Tomato and
Garlic Dip**

·

Tapénade

·

Devilled Crab Dip

·

Stilton and Walnut Dip

·

Hot Party Punch

·

Sparkling Celebration Cup

·

*I*f you're in the mood to invite a crowd but rather unsure about catering for a large number, a drinks party with an interesting selection of different dips and dunks is the perfect solution. An informal party like this does not involve hours of preparation: with the help of a food processor, dips can be whizzed up in seconds, and there's absolutely no cooking; even plates and cutlery are unnecessary. Dunks can be as imaginative as you dare – in fact the more unusual they are the more they will spark off conversation and get the party going. Arrange dips and dunks in small containers on trays around the room so that guests can get at them easily in small groups – this is much better than everyone crowding round one large table.

A fun idea to echo the bubbles in the sparkling drink is to decorate the ceiling of the party room with balloons. Balloons inflated with helium will 'float' on the ceiling and are especially effective if you crowd them closely together. Choose balloons of the same colour or mix two colours together and attach matching coloured streamers to them so that they dangle softly just above people's heads. For this party, a mixture of orange and red balloons and streamers would reflect the colours of both the food and drink with striking effect.

PIQUANT TOMATO AND GARLIC DIP

Using bread soaked in water to thicken this dip gives just the right consistency for dipping and dunking.

INGREDIENTS

three 50 g (2 oz) cans anchovies
100 ml (3½ fl oz/scant ½ cup) milk
50 g (2 oz) crustless white bread
2 tomatoes, skinned, seeded and chopped
2 garlic cloves, skinned and crushed
2 tablespoons wine vinegar
1 tablespoon tomato purée
300 ml (½ pint/1¼ cups) olive oil
freshly ground black pepper

Drain the anchovies, place in a bowl and cover with the milk. Leave to soak for 20 minutes.

Meanwhile, soak the white bread in cold water for a few minutes, then squeeze with your fingers.

Drain the anchovies, rinse under cold running water and pat dry. Work the anchovies, squeezed bread, tomatoes, garlic, wine vinegar and tomato purée in a blender or food processor. Add the oil, a drop at a time, and work the machine until the mixture thickens. Continue adding the oil in a thin, steady stream. When all the oil has been added, add pepper to taste and transfer the dip to a bowl. Cover and chill overnight.

To serve: let the dip come to room temperature for about 30 minutes, stir well and taste for seasoning. Turn into bowls.

TAPENADE

Drain the anchovies, place in a bowl and cover with the milk. Leave to soak for 20 minutes. Drain the anchovies, rinse under cold running water and pat dry.

Work the anchovies, olives, capers and mustard in a blender or food processor. Add the oil, a drop at a time, and work the machine until the mixture thickens. Continue adding the oil in a thin, steady stream as if making mayonnaise. When all the oil has been added, stir in lemon juice and pepper to taste. Transfer the dip to a bowl, cover tightly and chill in the refrigerator overnight.

To serve: let the dip come to room temperature for about 30 minutes, stir well and taste for seasoning. Turn into bowls and garnish with lemon slices and capers.

Tapénade originated in Provence (the Provençal word for capers is tapeno). Sometimes tuna fish is added, but both the Piquant Tomato and Garlic Dip and the Devilled Crab Dip are quite fishy, so the tuna has been omitted for this occasion.

INGREDIENTS

two 50 g (2 oz) cans anchovies

90 ml (6 tbsp) milk

225 g (8 oz/1⅓ cups) pitted black olives

3 tablespoons capers

2 teaspoons French mustard

250 ml (8 fl oz/1 cup) olive oil

1 tablespoon lemon juice, or to taste

freshly ground black pepper

TO GARNISH

lemon slices

capers

DEVILLED CRAB DIP

Put the crab meat into a bowl and stir well. Gradually stir in the mayonnaise until evenly mixed, then season with the remaining ingredients. Cover tightly and chill in the refrigerator overnight.

To serve: stir well and taste for seasoning. Turn into bowls and sprinkle with cayenne. Serve chilled.

When making the mayonnaise for this dip, use 2 egg yolks, 450 ml (¾ pint/2 cups) oil and seasonings to taste. Do not add lemon juice or wine vinegar as this will thin down the mayonnaise and make the consistency too runny.

INGREDIENTS

450 g (1 lb) packet frozen white and dark crab meat, defrosted

450 ml (¾ pint/2 cups) very thick homemade mayonnaise

2 teaspoons chilli sauce

2 teaspoons Worcestershire sauce

1 teaspoon garlic salt

½ teaspoon English mustard powder

cayenne pepper, to garnish

STILTON AND WALNUT DIP

Other blue cheeses can be used: Italian Gorgonzola or Dolcelatte are both excellent in dips because their creamy consistency makes them easy to blend smoothly. Take care when adding salt as most blue cheeses tend to be salty.

INGREDIENTS

225 g (½ lb) Blue Stilton cheese, at room temperature

175 g (6 oz/¾ cup) full-fat soft cheese (cream cheese)

225 g (8 oz/1 cup) carton Greek strained yogurt

100 g (4 oz/1 cup) walnut halves

2 teaspoons finely chopped fresh sage

salt

freshly ground black pepper

4–6 tablespoons milk

Remove the rind from the Stilton, then crumble the cheese into a blender or food processor. Add the soft cheese and yogurt and work to form a smooth mixture.

Finely chop about two-thirds of the walnuts. Add to the dip with the sage and salt and pepper to taste, then work again and add enough milk to give a creamy consistency. Transfer to a bowl, cover tightly and chill in the refrigerator overnight.

To serve: let the dip come to room temperature for about 30 minutes. Stir well, then taste for seasoning and thin down with a little milk if liked. Turn into bowls and garnish with the remaining walnut halves.

HOT PARTY PUNCH

Stud the oranges with the cloves and place in a baking dish. Bake at 180°C (350°F) mark 4 for 1 hour.

Cut the oranges into quarters and place in a large pan. Add the remaining ingredients and bring very slowly to just below boiling point. Remove from the heat, cover and leave to stand overnight.

To serve: strain the punch, then return to the rinsed-out pan. Heat through gently without boiling. If liked, transfer to a large heatproof serving bowl. Float orange slices on the top.

A preserving pan is ideal for making hot punches and mulled wines. Choose an inexpensive claret as it is perfectly good enough for making punches. Baking the whole oranges in the oven increases their juiciness.

INGREDIENTS

2 oranges
8 cloves
12 (70 cl) bottles red wine
200 ml (7 fl oz/scant 1 cup) Southern Comfort
two 5 cm (2 inch) cinnamon sticks
50 g (2 oz/¼ cup) caster (superfine) sugar
few drops of Angostura bitters
orange slices, to serve

SPARKLING CELEBRATION CUP

Pour the Southern Comfort into a large bowl, add the orange juice and ice cubes, then the cider. Stir briskly to mix. Float the raspberries on the top, with lemon balm or cucumber if liked. Serve immediately.

This cup needs to be made as and when guests are ready to be served as the bubbles in the cider quickly subside, so make up a quarter of the ingredients at a time. Sparkling cider, or pomagne, is inexpensive and perfectly adequate, but if you feel like splashing out for a celebration, why not try champagne?

INGREDIENTS

37 cl (½ bottle) Southern Comfort
strained juice of 4 oranges
ice cubes
5 (70 cl) bottles sparkling cider
450 g (1 lb) fresh or frozen raspberries
fresh lemon balm leaves or ½ cucumber, very thinly sliced (optional)

WEST COAST MENU

SERVES 6

·

Potato Skins

·

Red Hot Rib Stickers

·

**Spinach and Iceberg Salad
with Blue Cheese
and Walnuts**

·

**Squidgy
Chocolate Brownies**

·

*I*nvite your friends to this Californian-inspired meal around brunchtime – any time from eleven in the morning and, if weather permits, hold the party outside. In California, entertaining is frequently around the pool or at the beach, but on a bright sunny day the patio, lawn or balcony will suffice to capture the right mood. Help give your garden a sunny look with a yellow or yellow and white striped awning (which will also come in useful if you are unlucky enough to have rain), plus sun umbrellas and deckchairs in the same colours. Sunshine yellow tablecloths and napkins will also reflect the Californian look, with glasses and plates to match, although a mixture of blue and yellow will endorse the theme of sunny skies and shimmering blue seas. When guests arrive, get quickly into the Californian mood by serving glasses of Tequila Sunrise. Enlist a 'barman' to mix the cocktails individually in true American style, the recipe is simple – see page 101.

POTATO SKINS

Chopped crisply grilled bacon can be handed round in a separate bowl to be sprinkled over these skins. It provides a crunchy contrast to the accompanying creamy dip.

INGREDIENTS

6 baking potatoes

1 tablespoon groundnut or vegetable oil

salt

groundnut or vegetable oil, for deep frying

Scrub the potatoes clean, then dry them with absorbent kitchen paper. Roll in the oil and then in salt. Thread the potatoes on skewers and place directly on the oven shelf. Bake at 200°C (400°F) mark 6 for 1¼–1½ hours until the potatoes feel tender when squeezed.

Meanwhile, make the dip: mix the soured cream and yogurt together and sprinkle in the chives, salt and pepper to taste. Chill in the refrigerator until serving time.

When the potatoes are tender, remove from the oven and cut in half lengthways. Scoop out the flesh, leaving a thin layer next to the skin. Cut each skin in half lengthways again.

Heat the oil in a deep-fat fryer to 190°C (375°F). Deep fry the potato skins, a few at a time, for 30–60 seconds until crisp. Remove with a slotted spoon and drain upside down on absorbent kitchen paper.

To serve: sprinkle the potatoes with a little salt. Place the bowl of dip in the centre of a large platter and arrange the potato skins around it.

DIP
150 ml (¼ pint/⅔ cup) soured cream
150 ml (¼ pint/⅔ cup) Greek strained yogurt
snipped chives
freshly ground black pepper

RED HOT RIB STICKERS

Cut the pork into individual ribs if this has not already been done by the butcher. Divide the pork spareribs equally between 2 roasting tins.

Heat the remaining ingredients in a pan, stirring well to combine. Pour over the ribs. Roast at 200°C (400°F) mark 6 for 1 hour, swopping the tins over and turning the ribs occasionally to baste with the sauce.

Reduce the oven temperature to 180°C (350°F) mark 4 and continue roasting for a further 30 minutes or until the ribs are browned and the meat is very tender.

To serve: remove the ribs from the tins with tongs and place them on a warm large dish. Transfer the sauce to a pan on top of the cooker and boil to reduce, if liked. Spoon the sauce over the ribs.

American or Chinese-style spareribs are extremely more-ish cooked in this way. Check the ribs before buying – some are meatier than others and some are extremely fatty. Look for ribs with a good proportion of meat to bone.

INGREDIENTS
2 kg (4½ lb) pork spareribs
300 ml (½ pint/1¼ cups) chicken stock
6 tablespoons clear honey
6 tablespoons tomato ketchup
6 tablespoons Southern Comfort
4 tablespoons soft brown sugar
2 garlic cloves, skinned and crushed
3 tablespoons American mustard
3 tablespoons chilli sauce
2 teaspoons salt

SPINACH AND ICEBERG SALAD WITH BLUE CHEESE AND WALNUTS

The salad vegetables and dressing can be made in advance, then assembled at the last minute. Do not toss the salad until just before serving or the spinach and lettuce will go limp.

INGREDIENTS

225 g (½ lb) young fresh spinach leaves

½ Iceberg lettuce

100 g (¼ lb) Roquefort cheese

4 tablespoons walnut oil

1 tablespoon white wine vinegar

salt

freshly ground black pepper

75 g (3 oz/¾ cup) shelled walnuts, chopped

Wash the spinach thoroughly, cut off and discard the stalks. Dry the leaves on a clean teatowel. Wash the lettuce and cut into wedges.

Mash a third of the Roquefort in a bowl. Add the oil and vinegar with a little salt and plenty of black pepper. Whisk with a fork until well combined and thickened.

To serve: add the spinach and lettuce to the bowl and toss to coat lightly in the dressing. Crumble the remaining Roquefort over the top and sprinkle with the walnuts.

SQUIDGY CHOCOLATE BROWNIES

INGREDIENTS

120 ml (4 fl oz/½ cup) groundnut oil

225 g (8 oz/1⅓ cups) soft brown sugar

1 tablespoon Southern Comfort

2 eggs, beaten

50 g (2 oz/½ cup) plain (all-purpose) white flour

40 g (1½ oz/6 tablespoons) cocoa powder

1 teaspoon baking powder

¼ teaspoon salt

50 g (2 oz/½ cup) shelled walnuts, roughly chopped

Grease and line a shallow 23 cm (9 inch) square cake tin. Put the oil, sugar and Southern Comfort into a bowl and beat well to mix. Beat in the eggs.

Sift the flour, cocoa powder, baking powder and salt together, then stir into the mixture in the bowl. Fold in the nuts until evenly mixed.

Pour the mixture into the prepared tin. Bake at 180°C (350°F) mark 4 for 25–30 minutes until a skewer inserted in the cake comes out clean. Cool in the tin, then turn out, wrap and store in an airtight container for 24 hours.

To serve: unwrap and cut into 16 neat squares. Serve with scoops of vanilla ice cream.

*T*he crunchy texture of deep-fried
Potato Skins (page 28) is perfect
with a contrasting creamy dip,
and they can be handed round on a large platter for guests to help themselves.
Spinach and Iceberg Salad with Blue Cheese and Walnuts (page 30) is a
popular Californian combination.

SUMMER

There's no better time to entertain your friends than in the summer. Whenever you can, plan your party outside – this makes for an informal and relaxed atmosphere that both you and your guests can enjoy. Eating outside increases appetites, so your friends will appreciate your culinary efforts even more than usual.

MISSISSIPPI MENU

SERVES 6–8

·

Scarlett O'Hara

·

Cajun 'Blackened' Fish

·

Chicken and Seafood Jambalaya

·

Chocolate Pecan Pie

·

*L*iven up your cookery repertoire with this unusual menu for an informal buffet meal. Hot and spicy, it's a mixture of Cajun and Creole, two cooking cults that are sweeping the States. Cajun is a combination of French Canadian and southern cooking – created by the French Canadians when they settled in Louisiana in the late eighteenth century; Creole originated in the French colonies of New Orleans, but has since been influenced by settlers from Spain. Both styles of cooking are colourful, exotic and punchy, so be as flamboyant as you possibly dare. Use hot, vibrant colours for table-cloths and table decorations – red is the obvious choice, but orange, yellow, purple and brilliant pink can also be used, and mixed together they have an electric effect. An inexpensive way to decorate the room is to ruche folded squares of brilliant coloured tissue paper close together and hang them like paper chains from the ceiling or as garlands on the walls or around the edge of the table. Brightly coloured streamers would give a similar if less dramatic effect and New Orleans jazz would set the right mood from the start. If you can persuade your friends to wear striped trousers and waistcoats they'll look the part!

SCARLETT O'HARA

Put the Southern Comfort, cranberry juice and crushed ice in a shaker and shake until thoroughly mixed. Strain into a cocktail glass and curl the strips of lime zest over the rim. Serve immediately.

Note: If preferred, you can mix several drinks at a time in a blender, as they do in some cocktail bars.

No prizes for guessing why this cocktail has this name! Cranberry juice is difficult to obtain outside the United States, but you can use cranberry and raspberry juice or cranberry and apple, both of which are available ready-mixed in bottles at many large supermarkets. (Cranberry and raspberry is sweeter than the cranberry and apple.) This quantity is for one cocktail, which should be made in a cocktail shaker.

INGREDIENTS

37.5 ml (1½ fl oz/2½ tablespoons) Southern Comfort

120–175 ml (4–6 fl oz/½–¾ cup) cranberry juice

crushed ice

1 strip of thinly pared lime zest, to serve

CAJUN 'BLACKENED' FISH

Crush the peppercorns and allspice in a mortar and pestle, then mix with the cayenne pepper and garlic salt. Rub this mixture into the flesh side of the fish. Place in a single layer in a large dish and spoon over the melted butter. Cover and chill in the refrigerator for 2 hours.

Place a heavy cast iron frying pan (skillet) over moderate heat for 10–15 minutes until very hot. Increase the heat, add 2–3 pieces of fish, skin side down, and cook for 3 minutes until the butter begins to brown. Turn the fish over and cook on the other side for the same length of time. Remove from the pan and keep hot. Repeat with the remaining fish.

To serve: arrange the fish on a warm platter and garnish with lemon slices or wedges.

Ask your fishmonger for the thickest part of the cod from the centre of the fillet and try to get even-sized pieces.

INGREDIENTS

60 black peppercorns

12 whole allspice berries

4 teaspoons cayenne pepper

2 teaspoons garlic salt

6–8 thick pieces of cod fillet

100 g (4 oz/1 stick) unsalted butter, melted

lemon slices or wedges, to garnish

CHICKEN AND SEAFOOD JAMBALAYA

Oysters are frequently used in authentic Creole jambalaya recipes. Here, mussels are suggested as they are more widely available, cheaper and more readily accepted. This recipe requires a whole chicken to be chopped into pieces including bones. This gives a sweet and juicy jambalaya, but if you prefer to use cubes of boneless breast meat – you will need about 700 g (1½ lb).

INGREDIENTS

450 g (1 lb) unpeeled prawns (shrimp)

2 tablespoons olive oil

100 g (¼ lb) smoked ham, cubed

100 g (¼ lb) chorizo, sliced

2 medium onions, skinned and finely chopped

2 garlic cloves, skinned and finely chopped

4 spring onions (scallions), trimmed and chopped

3 celery stalks, trimmed and chopped

1 green pepper, cored, seeded and chopped

1.6 kg (3½ lb) chicken, skinned and chopped into 5 cm (2 inch) pieces

2 bay leaves

1 teaspoon cayenne pepper

1 teaspoon dried oregano

1 teaspoon dried thyme

salt

freshly ground black pepper

6 tomatoes, chopped

450 g (1 lb) easy-cook long grain rice

700 g (1½ lb) fresh mussels in their shells, scrubbed

Peel 350 g (¾ lb) of the prawns and set aside. Put the shells in a saucepan and pour over 750 ml (1¼ pints/3 cups) water. Bring to the boil, lower the heat, cover and simmer for 15 minutes. Strain the stock and reserve.

Heat the oil in a large flameproof casserole, add the ham and chorizo and stir fry for 5 minutes until slightly crisp. Add the onions, garlic, spring onions, celery and green pepper and cook for 5 minutes, stirring constantly.

Add the chicken, increase the heat to high and cook for 1 minute, turning the chicken pieces constantly. Reduce the heat to moderate and add the bay leaves, cayenne, oregano, thyme, 1 teaspoon salt and pepper to taste. Cook for 8 minutes, stirring constantly.

Add the tomatoes and cook for 2 minutes. Stir in the rice and pour over 600 ml (1 pint/2½ cups) of the reserved prawn stock. Bring to the boil, lower the heat, cover and cook for 15 minutes. Remove the lid, stir in the peeled prawns and mussels and more prawn stock if necessary. Cover again and cook for a further 5–10 minutes or until all the mussels are open and most of the liquid has been absorbed.

To serve: taste for seasoning, then turn into a warm dish and garnish with the remaining unpeeled prawns.

*E*or an informal supper party with
a difference, Chicken and Seafood
Jambalaya (above) is the ideal
main course. Guests can help themselves to the colourful combination of
chicken, mussels, prawns (shrimp), ham and chorizo cooked in a hot and spicy
mixture of fresh vegetables and rice.

CHOCOLATE PECAN PIE

Pecan nuts are native to the Mississippi valley; their flavour is somewhat like walnuts, but pecans are oilier. Look for pecans in health food shops and some delicatessens. Walnuts can be substituted if pecans prove difficult to obtain.

PASTRY

275 g (10 oz/2½ cups) plain (all-purpose) white flour

3 tablespoons good-quality cocoa powder

pinch of salt

150 g (5 oz/1 stick plus 2 tablespoons) unsalted butter, diced

2 tablespooons caster (superfine) sugar

FILLING

200 g (7 oz/1¾ cups) shelled pecan nuts

3 eggs, beaten

225 g (8 oz/1⅓ cups) light soft brown sugar

250 ml (8 fl oz/1 cup) evaporated milk

1 teaspoon vanilla essence (extract)

50 g (2 oz/½ stick) unsalted butter, melted

300 ml (½ pint/1¼ cups) double (heavy) cream, to finish

Make the pastry: sift the flour, cocoa powder and salt into a large bowl. Add the diced butter and rub in with the fingertips until the mixture resembles coarse breadcrumbs. Stir in the sugar. Gradually add 2–3 tablespoons cold water until the dough begins to hold together (it will still be quite crumbly). Turn out on to a lightly floured surface, shape into a ball, then roll out and use to line a lightly greased 25.5 cm (10 inch) fluted flan tin with a removable base. Prick all over with a fork, then chill in the refrigerator for 1 hour.

Line the pastry with foil and fill with baking beans. Bake blind at 190°C (375°F) mark 5 for 10 minutes. Remove the foil and beans, return the pastry case to the oven and bake for a further 5 minutes. Remove from the oven and leave to cool. Reduce the oven temperature to 170°C (325°F) mark 3.

Meanwhile, make the filling: chop the pecans, reserving 50 g (2 oz/½ cup) well-formed halves for the decoration. Put the chopped nuts in a bowl and add the remaining filling ingredients. Mix well and pour into the pastry case. Bake for 50–55 minutes or until set in the centre. Leave to cool.

To serve: carefully remove the sides of the tin and place the pie on a plate. Whip the cream until it holds its shape, then swirl over the top of the pie. Decorate with the reserved pecans.

DEMI-VEG DINNER

Surprise your friends and salute the new demi-veg craze with this delicious and nutritious three course meal. Demi-veg is the fashionable, sophisticated diet of the moment. It's not cranky or faddy, just a sensible way of eating that cuts down on fats – especially the saturated fats found in red meat. Demi-veggies eat mostly crisp and crunchy fresh fruit and vegetables, pulses, grains and nuts, although they do eat fish, eggs and white meat in moderation and low-fat dairy produce. This fresh and colourful menu will quickly dispel all those preconceived ideas your friends might have about the "nut cutlet" vegetarian brigade. Keep the table simple but stylish, with a designer or high tech theme. Dramatic black and white china will show off the jewel-bright colours of the food, with silver, chrome or stainless steel cutlery setting a sophisticated style. Candles will give shimmer and white candles in black holders arranged together with black candles in white holders at each place setting will look sensational. To drink, serve Margarita cocktails in black glasses with frosty white salted rims and black or white swizzle-sticks.

SERVES 4

·

Chèvrettes

·

Spicy Spinach Roulade
with
Pine Nut Pilaf

·

Barbecued Bananas

·

CHEVRETTES

Cut each chèvre in half horizontally. Spread the flour out on a sheet of greaseproof (waxed) paper and add pepper to taste. Coat the pieces of cheese in the flour, brushing off the excess.

Beat the egg in a bowl. Spread the sesame seeds out on another sheet of greaseproof paper. Dip the pieces of cheese in the egg, brush until evenly coated, then coat in the sesame seeds. Chill in the refrigerator for at least 30 minutes.

Put the cheeses on a lightly oiled baking sheet. Bake at 200°C (400°F) mark 6 for 8–10 minutes until hot (the centres should feel soft when squeezed gently).

To serve: transfer to individual plates with a fish slice (pancake turner) and garnish with radicchio or endive.

Barrel-shaped goats' cheeses are sold individually wrapped in supermarkets and delicatessens. If the cheese is chilled when it goes into the oven, it will cook perfectly so that when it is cut, the centre oozes out.

INGREDIENTS

two 100 g (4 oz) ripe chèvre (goat's cheese), at room temperature
1 tablespoon plain (all-purpose) white flour
freshly ground black pepper
1 egg, size 5 or 6 (medium)
6–7 tablespoons sesame seeds
radicchio or endive (red lettuce or chicory), to serve

*F*or dramatic impact, serve
individual slices of Spicy Spinach
Roulade (page 40) on classy
black plates (right). Pine Nut Pilaf (page 41) is a substantial
accompaniment, but be sure to serve a seasonal salad as well. Barbecued
Bananas (page 41) look good on the individual leaf-shaped dishes.

SPICY SPINACH ROULADE

Everything can be prepared for this roulade in advance of your dinner party, up to the point where the egg whites are beaten. This part of the method must be left until just before you are ready to bake the roulade or the egg whites will lose their bulk. It is important to chop the mushrooms and prawns finely or the filling will be difficult to spread and the roulade awkward to roll.

INGREDIENTS

900 g (2 lb) fresh spinach

salt

1 teaspoon mustard seeds

1 teaspoon coriander seeds

½ teaspoon cumin seeds

225 g (8 oz/1 cup) low-fat soft cheese (cream cheese)

4 eggs, separated

freshly ground black pepper

15 g (½ oz/1 tablespoon) butter

175 g (6 oz/1½ cups) button mushrooms, wiped and finely chopped

1 teaspoon turmeric

225 g (8 oz/1⅓ cups) peeled cooked prawns (shrimp), defrosted and thoroughly dried, finely chopped

TO GARNISH

unpeeled prawns (shrimp)

parsley sprig

Line a greased 33×23 cm (13×9 inch) Swiss roll tin (jelly roll pan) with non-stick baking parchment. Set aside.

Wash the spinach thoroughly until clean. Remove and discard the stalks. Put the leaves in a large saucepan with only the water that clings to them. Add salt to taste and cook over gentle heat for 5 minutes, shaking the pan constantly, until the spinach wilts and shrinks. Drain well.

Turn the spinach into a blender or food processor and work to a purée. Crush the spices with a mortar and pestle, then add to the spinach with half of the cheese. Work again in the machine until evenly mixed. Add the egg yolks and salt and pepper to taste and work again until smooth. Transfer to a large bowl.

Melt the butter in a medium pan, add the mushrooms and turmeric and toss over high heat until the juices have evaporated. Add the prawns and heat through. Turn the mixture into a bowl, add the remaining cheese and salt and pepper to taste. Beat to a soft, spreading consistency. Cover and keep warm.

Whisk the egg whites in a clean bowl until standing in stiff peaks. Fold into the spinach mixture, then immediately spread over the parchment with a palette knife (metal spatula). Bake at 200°C (400°F) mark 6 for 15 minutes or until firm to the touch. Turn the roulade out on to a large sheet of baking parchment and carefully peel off the lining paper. Immediately spread with the prawn mixture. Roll up carefully with the help of the parchment.

To serve: lift the roulade carefully on to a warm serving plate and place seam side down. Garnish the top of the roulade with prawns and parsley.

PINE NUT PILAF

Melt 50 g (2 oz/4 tablespoons) of the butter with the oil in a heavy saucepan, add the onion and cook gently, stirring frequently, for about 10 minutes, until soft but not coloured.

Add the cardamom pods and rice, stir to coat in the butter, then pour in the stock. Add salt and pepper to taste and bring to the boil, stirring. Lower the heat, cover tightly and simmer very gently for 15 minutes or until the rice is tender. Remove from the heat.

To serve: remove the cardamom pods which will have risen to the surface of the rice, then stir in the nuts and raisins, with the remaining butter. Taste for seasoning.

To remove excess starch from basmati rice, put the rice in a sieve, pick over to remove any stones, then rinse under cold water until it runs clear. Put in a bowl, cover with cold water and leave to soak for 20 minutes. Drain well.

INGREDIENTS

65 g (2½ oz/5 tablespoons) butter

1 tablespoon olive, groundnut or vegetable oil

1 medium onion, skinned and finely chopped

6 cardamom pods, bruised

350 g (12 oz/1¾ cups) basmati rice, rinsed and soaked

450 ml (¾ pint/2 cups) hot chicken stock

salt

freshly ground black pepper

100 g (4 oz/1 cup) pine nuts

50 g (2 oz/⅓ cup) raisins

BARBECUED BANANAS

Put all the ingredients (except the bananas and orange slices) in a pan and stir over gentle heat until the sugar has dissolved.

Cut 4 large rectangles of foil. Peel the bananas and place one on each piece of foil. Prick them in several places with a fine skewer, then pour over the sauce.

Bring the 2 long sides of the foil up over each banana, then fold the join over several times to seal thoroughly. Fold up the short ends of the foil so that the juices cannot run out during cooking.

Place the parcels in a baking dish or roasting tin. Bake at 190°C (375°F) mark 5 for 15 minutes.

To serve: open the parcels carefully and transfer the bananas to individual dishes. Pour over the juices which have collected in the foil and decorate with orange slices. Serve hot.

These bananas can be wrapped in their foil parcels several hours in advance of your dinner party, then all you have to do is pop them into the preheated oven just as you are sitting down to the main course.

INGREDIENTS

4 tablespoons Southern Comfort

50 g (2 oz/¼ cup) demerara (brown granulated) sugar

finely grated rind and juice of 1 large orange

juice of 1 lemon

½ teaspoon ground cinnamon

25 g (1 oz/¼ stick) butter

4 ripe bananas

orange slices, to decorate

BRING A DISH

SERVES 6

·

Pâté of Chicken Livers

·

Pork and Pineapple Casserole

·

Strawberry and Orange Mousse

·

*T*ake the effort out of entertaining by organizing a 'bring a dish' party. Get together a group of friends and split the preparation, cooking and expense between you. It's great fun as it takes the pressure off and lets everyone relax and enjoy themselves. This three course menu is really simple to organize. One person or couple can make the starter, another the main course and a third the dessert. For practical reasons it's best if the actual host or hostess provides the accompaniments such as crisp rolls or toast for the pâté, salad and rice or noodles for the main course.

Try to keep the table setting as simple as possible with white or a neutral colour for the background. This way it will not matter so much about the colour or style of the dishes your friends bring. As you will have less to do than usual in the way of cooking you can take more time over the table. Make menu cards for each place setting and matching place names, arrange a small posy of flowers on each side plate and fold the napkins decoratively. And for a special treat, serve an individual boxed chocolate to each guest with the coffee and liqueurs.

PATE OF CHICKEN LIVERS

Tubs of frozen chicken livers, available from supermarkets and freezer centres, are most convenient for making this type of pâté.

INGREDIENTS

175 g (6 oz/1½ sticks) unsalted butter

2 shallots, skinned and roughly chopped

1 garlic clove, skinned and roughly chopped

450 g (1 lb) chicken livers

4 tablespoons Southern Comfort

225 g (8 oz/1 cup) full-fat soft cheese (cream cheese)

2 tablespoons finely chopped fresh oregano or 2 teaspoons dried

salt

freshly ground black pepper

TO GARNISH

fresh oregano

peppercorns

Melt 25 g (1 oz/¼ stick) of the butter in a heavy frying pan (skillet), add the shallots and cook gently, stirring frequently, for about 5 minutes until soft but not coloured. Add the garlic and fry for 1–2 minutes more, stirring constantly. Stir in another 25 g (1 oz/¼ stick) of the butter and the chicken livers and fry for 8–10 minutes until the livers are still just pink in the centre. Add the Southern Comfort and stir to blend with the livers.

Transfer the contents of the pan to a blender or food processor and work until well broken up. Add the cheese, oregano and salt and pepper to taste. Melt a further 50 g (2 oz/½ stick) butter, add to the machine and work again until evenly mixed.

Transfer the pâté to a serving dish and smooth the surface. Leave until cold. Melt the remaining butter gently in a clean pan and pour over the top of the pâté. Leave until cold, then cover tightly and chill in the refrigerator for at least 2 hours, overnight if possible.

To serve: uncover and arrange oregano and peppercorns on top of the melted butter as a garnish.

*C*risp rolls are the
perfect
accompaniment for
this rich and creamy Pâté of Chicken
Livers (left), although you could
serve hot toast if you prefer. The
beautiful decoration of strawberries
and cream (above) on top of the
Strawberry and Orange Mousse
(page 45) is best left until last.

PORK AND PINEAPPLE CASSEROLE

Cooking juices always thicken on standing; this casserole is made with extra liquid to allow for overnight standing and reheating. If you prefer thicker juices after reheating, simple remove the meat with a slotted spoon and boil the liquid rapidly on top of the cooker until reduced.

INGREDIENTS

15 g (½ oz/1 tablespoon) butter

2 tablespoons groundnut or vegetable oil

1.4–1.6 kg (3–3½ lb) boneless pork shoulder (sparerib), trimmed of excess fat and cut into cubes

4 tablespoons Southern Comfort

2 tablespoons dark soft brown sugar

2 teaspoons tomato purée

300 ml (½ pint/1¼ cups) unsweetened pineapple juice

300 ml (½ pint/1¼ cups) chicken stock

¼ teaspoon Tabasco (hot pepper) sauce, or to taste

salt

freshly ground black pepper

TO SERVE

15 g (½ oz/1 tablespoon) butter

1 tablespoon groundnut or vegetable oil

1 small red pepper, cored, seeded and sliced into thin rings

2 slices of fresh pineapple, cut into neat pieces

Melt the butter with the oil in a flameproof casserole, add the pork in batches and fry over moderate to high heat until golden brown on all sides.

Return all the meat to the casserole and stir in the Southern Comfort, sugar and tomato purée. Mix well, then pour in the pineapple juice and stock. Bring to the boil, stirring, and add the Tabasco and salt and pepper to taste. Cover tightly. Cook at 150°C (300°F) mark 2 for 1½ hours until the pork is tender, stirring occasionally. Leave in a cold place overnight.

To serve: reheat at 190°C (375°F) mark 5 for 20 minutes or until bubbling. Melt the butter with the oil in a heavy frying pan (skillet), add the red pepper rings and toss over high heat for a few minutes until softened. Add the pineapple pieces and heat through. Remove both pepper and pineapple with a slotted spoon and drain on absorbent kitchen paper. Taste the casserole for seasoning, then transfer to a warm serving dish and garnish with the red pepper and pineapple.

STRAWBERRY AND ORANGE MOUSSE

Hull and thinly slice enough strawberries to line the sides of a 2.3 litre (4 pint/5 pint) shallow glass dish. Hull half of the remaining strawberries and put into a blender or food processor with the orange rind and juice and the icing sugar. Work to a purée, then pass through a nylon sieve. Reserve the remaining strawberries for decoration.

Whisk the egg yolks and caster sugar together in a bowl until thick and light. Gradually whisk in the strawberry purée.

Sprinkle the gelatine over 3 tablespoons water in a small bowl and leave until spongy. Stand the bowl in a saucepan of hot water and heat gently until dissolved. Leave to cool, then stir into the mousse mixture.

Lightly whip the creams together in a large bowl. Fold a third into the mousse; cover the remaining cream and keep in the refrigerator.

Whisk the egg whites until stiff and fold into the mousse. Turn carefully into the strawberry-lined dish and chill in the refrigerator for 2–3 hours until set.

To serve: pipe the reserved cream around the edge of the mousse and place the remaining strawberries in the centre.

Strawberries and oranges make perfect partners, but you may use lime rind and juice instead of orange with equally good effect.

INGREDIENTS

700 g (1½ lb) fresh strawberries
finely grated rind of 1 large orange
5 tablespoons freshly squeezed orange juice
3 tablespoons icing (confectioners') sugar
3 egg yolks
100 g (4 oz/½ cup) caster (superfine) sugar
3 teaspoons gelatine (unflavored gelatin)
300 ml (½ pint/1¼ cups) double (heavy) cream
150 ml (¼ pint/⅔ cup) single (light) cream
2 egg whites

MIDSUMMER NIGHT BARBECUE PARTY

SERVES 8–10
·
Chilled Courgette (Zucchini) Soup with Blue Cheese
·
Lamb Brochettes
·
Surf 'n' Turf
·
Beefsteaks Teriyaki
·
Chicken Satay
·
Strawberry Meringue Glacé
·

*W*hen the night air is heady with the scent of summer flowers, invite your friends to join you in a celebration of the longest day. A barbecue party in the garden is one of the most informal ways to entertain, and with this menu of marinated meats and fish, a starter and a dessert that can be made well in advance, nothing could be more relaxed.

Pay particular attention to the lighting for an evening barbecue as even on the longest day you will be surprised how quickly the light fails. One of the prettiest ways to light a garden is to string Christmas tree fairy lights or lanterns through trees and bushes and along walls or fences. Special garden flare torches give a more dramatic effect and so too do hallogen spotlights. Or, as the sun finally fades from the garden, light candles, protecting them from any night breezes, and let your guests linger over the good food and wine by romantic candlelight.

CHILLED COURGETTE (ZUCCHINI) SOUP

INGREDIENTS

25 g (1 oz/¼ stick) butter
2 tablespoons olive oil
2 small onions, skinned and roughly chopped
1.4 kg (3 lb) courgettes (zucchini), trimmed and thinly sliced
2 litres (3½ pints/4½ pints) vegetable stock
350 g (¾ lb) blue cheese (Gorgonzola, Stilton, Dolcelatte), rind removed
salt
freshly ground black pepper

TO SERVE

300 ml (½ pint/1¼ cups) whipping cream, lightly whipped
chopped fresh herbs

Melt the butter with the oil in a large heavy saucepan, add the onions and cook gently, stirring frequently for about 5 minutes until soft but not coloured. Add the courgettes and stir to mix with the onion. Place a sheet of dampened greaseproof (waxed) paper directly on top of the vegetables. Cover the pan tightly with a lid and cook over very gentle heat for 15 minutes, shaking the pan occasionally.

Remove the lid and greaseproof paper, pour in the stock and bring to the boil, stirring. Lower the heat, crumble in the cheese, then add salt and pepper to taste. Half cover with the lid and simmer for 20 minutes until the courgettes are tender.

Slightly cool the soup and purée in batches in a blender or food processor until very smooth. Transfer the soup to a large bowl. Leave until cold, then cover and chill overnight.

To serve: stir well and taste for seasoning. Pour into bowls, swirl in cream, feather with a skewer and sprinkle with herbs.

LAMB BROCHETTES

Cut the lamb into 4 cm (1½ inch) cubes, including some of the fat so that the meat will be moist when cooked.

Whisk the wine, olive oil and lemon juice in a bowl with the crushed tomatoes and garlic. Add the cubes of lamb, chopped herbs and pepper to taste and stir well to mix. Cover the bowl and leave to marinate in the refrigerator overnight.

When ready to cook, halve the peppers lengthways and remove the cores and seeds. Cut the flesh into cubes. Thread the lamb and pepper cubes on to lightly oiled metal kebab skewers, alternating the colours of the pepper as attractively as possible.

Place the sprigs of herbs on the grid of a preheated barbecue. Place the skewers on top of the herbs and cook for 15–20 minutes. Turn the skewers frequently and brush with the marinade.

Make the garden heady with the scent of herbs when these brochettes are put on the barbecue on top of rosemary and marjoram sprigs. Succulent and juicy nuggets of lamb with traffic-light squares of pepper, they make the most eye-catching barbecue food.

INGREDIENTS

1.4 kg (3 lb) boneless shoulder of lamb

100 ml (3½ fl oz/scant ½ cup) red wine

100 ml (3½ fl oz/scant ½ cup) olive oil

juice of 2 lemons

2 large ripe tomatoes, skinned and crushed

3 garlic cloves, skinned and crushed

4 teaspoons chopped fresh rosemary

2 teaspoons chopped fresh marjoram

freshly ground black pepper

3 large peppers (red, green and yellow)

sprigs of fresh rosemary

sprigs of fresh marjoram

SURF 'N' TURF

A delicious American classic –
steak and shellfish cooked together
over hot coals. A clever
combination and an exciting taste
sensation.

INGREDIENTS

700 g (1½ lb) fillet (tenderloin)
steak

8–10 (bay) scallops, off the shell

6 tablespoons groundnut or
vegetable oil

finely grated rind and juice of
3 limes

6 tablespoons Southern Comfort

freshly ground black pepper

16–20 raw 'Mediterranean' prawns
(jumbo shrimp)

Cut the fillet steak into 4 cm (1½ inch) cubes. Cut each scallop in half. Whisk the oil in a bowl with the lime rind and juice, the Southern Comfort and plenty of pepper to taste. Add the steak and scallops and mix gently. Cover the bowl and leave to marinate in the refrigerator overnight.

When ready to cook, thread 16–20 lightly oiled metal kebab skewers with the steak and scallops, then thread a prawn on the end of each one. Place the skewers on the grid of a preheated barbecue. Cook for 8–10 minutes, turning frequently and brushing with the marinade.

BEEFSTEAKS TERIYAKI

Give an oriental touch to your
barbecue party with these
Japanese-style steaks. Teriyaki
sauce is pungently sweet and is
equally delicious with other meats
such as chicken and pork – and
with fish and shellfish as well.

INGREDIENTS

8–10 sirloin or entrecôte steaks

7.5 cm (3 inch) piece of fresh root
ginger, skinned and roughly
chopped

3 garlic cloves, skinned

6 black peppercorns

150 ml (¼ pint/⅔ cup) sake
(Japanese rice wine) or sweet
sherry

200 ml (7 fl oz/⅞ cup) shoyu
(Japanese soy sauce)

4 tablespoons caster (superfine)
sugar

6 tablespoons groundnut or
vegetable oil

Trim excess fat off the steaks. Crush the ginger, garlic and peppercorns together in a mortar and pestle. Transfer to a bowl and whisk in the sake or sherry, shoyu and sugar.

Place the steaks in one or more shallow dishes and slowly pour over the marinade. Cover loosely and leave to marinate for at least 24, preferably 48, hours. Turn the steaks in the marinade as often as possible during this time.

When ready to cook, remove the steaks from the marinade one at a time and brush one side with oil. Place the steaks on the grid of a preheated barbecue. Cook for 12–15 minutes, turning once. Mix the remaining oil with the marinade and brush frequently over the steaks during cooking.

CHICKEN SATAY

Skin the chicken breasts and cut the flesh into 1 cm (½ inch) cubes. Dry fry the cumin and coriander seeds in a heavy frying pan (skillet) for a few minutes, shaking the pan constantly. Remove from the heat and crush in a mortar and pestle.

Put the onion and garlic in a blender or food processor with the soy sauce, lime or lemon juice, sugar and turmeric. Add the dry-fried spices and work for a few seconds until well mixed. Transfer to a bowl, add the chicken pieces and stir well. Cover the bowl and leave to marinate in the refrigerator overnight.

When ready to cook, soak the bamboo skewers in warm water for 30 minutes. Drain, then thread with the chicken pieces.

Make the peanut sauce: put the coconut in a blender or food processor, pour in 450 ml (¾ pint/2 cups) boiling water and work for 5 seconds. Turn into a sieve placed over a bowl and press with the back of a metal spoon to extract as much 'milk' as possible. Set aside.

Heat the oil in a heavy saucepan, add the onion and garlic and cook gently for about 5 minutes, stirring frequently, until soft but not coloured. Add the coconut milk and the remaining sauce ingredients and bring to the boil, stirring constantly. Lower the heat and simmer until thick, stirring frequently. Pour into a serving bowl or jug. Garnish with the lime shreds.

Place the skewers on the grid of a preheated barbecue. Cook for about 10 minutes, turning the skewers frequently and brushing with oil. Hand the peanut sauce separately.

Indonesian spicy satay sticks served with a pungent peanut sauce add an exotic interest to the barbecue. Buy authentic bamboo skewers from an oriental supermarket or specialist kitchen shop – you will need 24–30 skewers for this recipe.

INGREDIENTS

8 boned chicken breasts

1 teaspoon cumin seeds

1 teaspoon coriander seeds

1 small onion, skinned and roughly chopped

2 garlic cloves, skinned and roughly chopped

6 tablespoons soy sauce

4 tablespoons lime or lemon juice

2 teaspoons dark soft brown sugar

1 teaspoon turmeric

peanut oil, for brushing

lime shreds, to garnish

PEANUT SAUCE

225 g (8 oz/2⅔ cups) desiccated (shredded) coconut

3 tablespoons peanut oil

1 medium onion, skinned and chopped

2 garlic cloves, skinned and chopped

100 g (4 oz/½ cup) crunchy peanut butter

2 tablespoons lime or lemon juice

2 tablespoons dark soft brown sugar

2 teaspoons chilli powder

1 teaspoon salt

*T*he delicate feathering of cream and light sprinkling of fresh herbs (above) give a professional touch to Chilled Courgette (Zucchini) Soup with Blue Cheese (page 46) that is bound to impress your guests right from the start. Follow with the medley of marinated barbecued meat and fish (opposite), plus a selection of rice and raw vegetable salads.

STRAWBERRY MERINGUE GLACE

Strawberries are a must for midsummer and nothing can set them off better than meringue and ice cream. For 8–10 people, you will need to make two meringues.

INGREDIENTS

4 egg whites, size 1 or 2 (large)

225 g (8 oz/1¾ cups) icing (confectioners') sugar

700 g (1½ lb) small fresh strawberries

4 tablespoons Southern Comfort

finely grated rind and juice of 1 large orange

300 ml (½ pint/1¼ cups) good-quality vanilla ice cream

With a pencil, mark a 23 cm (9 inch) circle on a sheet of non-stick baking parchment, using a dinner plate as a guide. Turn the paper over and place on a baking sheet. Set aside.

Put the egg whites in a deep bowl. Sift in the icing sugar. Stand the bowl over a saucepan half full of gently simmering water and whisk vigorously with a hand-held electric whisk until the meringue will stand in stiff peaks. Remove the bowl from the pan of water.

Spread a third of the meringue over the marked circle on the baking parchment. Spoon the remainder into a piping (pastry) bag fitted with a star nozzle (tube) and pipe a double row of rosettes around the edge of the circle. Bake at 100°C (200°F) mark low for about 2½ hours until crisp and dry. Transfer the meringue on the parchment to a wire rack. Leave to cool.

Meanwhile, hull three-quarters of the strawberries and place in a bowl. Pour over the Southern Comfort, add the orange rind and juice and fold gently to mix. Cover and chill in the refrigerator until serving time.

To serve: carefully peel the parchment off the meringue and place the meringue on a serving plate or cake stand. With a slotted spoon, remove about a third of the strawberries from the juice and arrange inside the edge of the meringue case. Place scoops of ice cream in the centre, then decorate with the reserved whole strawberries. Serve immediately, with the remaining strawberries handed separately in a bowl.

EVERYTHING RAW

*R*aw food is classy and cool, just the thing for summer entertaining buffet-style. When the weather's hot, appetites are jaded. Raw food provides a refreshing new taste experience. With this kind of party, the food itself will be the main talking point, and with dishes from Spain, Sweden, France, Italy and Mexico it is best to keep to cool, classic white for the buffet table itself, with may be a touch of pale pink to echo the colour of the marinated meats and fish. Position the table near open doors leading to the garden so that guests can help themselves before moving out into the open air. A white damask cloth and napkins always looks elegant and fresh with classic cutlery, including fish knives and forks if you have them. Keep the table as uncluttered as possible and encourage guests to try one dish at a time in order to savour individual flavours. Chilled dry white wine or champagne are the best drinks to have with raw food, or spritzers made from 3 parts dry white wine to 2 parts sparkling mineral water or soda.

SERVES 10

·

Gazpacho

·

Gravad Lax

·

Steak Tartare

·

Carpaccio

·

Ceviche

·

GAZPACHO

Mix together the green peppers, cucumber, tomatoes, onions and garlic. Work in batches in a blender or food processor. Transfer to a bowl and mix in the tomato juice, oil, wine vinegar and tomato purée. Work in batches again in the blender or food processor to make a smooth purée.

Strain the purée through a sieve into a clean bowl and add salt and pepper to taste. Cover the bowl and chill in the refrigerator overnight.

To serve: whisk the soup and taste for seasoning, then pour into a large bowl or tureen. Add ice cubes and serve immediately, with the croûtons and diced green pepper in separate bowls.

Guests should help themselves to the accompaniments, sprinkling them over their individual servings.

INGREDIENTS

225 g (½ lb) green peppers, cored, seeded and roughly chopped

1 large cucumber, roughly chopped

900 g (2 lb) ripe tomatoes, roughly chopped

100 g (4 oz/1 cup) Spanish (yellow) onions, skinned and roughly chopped

2 garlic cloves, skinned and roughly chopped

two 425 g (15 oz) cans tomato juice

5 tablespoons olive oil

5 tablespoons white wine vinegar

3 tablespoons tomato purée

salt

freshly ground black pepper

TO SERVE

ice cubes

croûtons

diced green pepper

*C*ool and refreshing Gazpacho
(page 53) is the ideal soup for hot
summer weather, while the
Swedish Gravad Lax (page 56) pictured opposite will impress your guests
with its stylish presentation.

GRAVAD LAX

Ask your fishmonger for the tail end of a whole salmon; he will most likely charge you less per kg (lb) than for the thick centre fillet. Salmon trout, which is less expensive than salmon, can also be used.

INGREDIENTS

1 tablespoon caster (superfine) sugar

1 tablespoon salt

1 tablespoon black peppercorns, coarsely crushed

4–6 tablespoons chopped fresh dill or 1–2 tablespoons dried dillweed

about 700 g (1½ lb) fresh salmon, filleted into 2 pieces

lemon slices, to garnish

MUSTARD AND DILL SAUCE

1 egg yolk

2 tablespoons German mustard

½ teaspoon sugar

salt

freshly ground black pepper

150 ml (¼ pint/⅔ cup) olive oil

2 tablespoons red wine vinegar

2 teaspoons chopped fresh dill or 1 teaspoon dried dillweed

Mix the sugar, salt, peppercorns and dill together in a bowl. Sprinkle a quarter of this mixture in a shallow (non-metal) dish. Put one fillet of the salmon, skin side down, in the dish. Sprinkle over half of the remaining mixture, then place the second salmon fillet on top, skin side uppermost. Sprinkle with the remaining mixture and rub it well into the skin. Cover the salmon with foil and place heavy weights on top. Refrigerate for 2–5 days, turning the salmon once every day and basting with the brine that collects in the bottom of the dish.

On the day of serving, make the sauce: put the egg yolk, mustard, sugar and salt and pepper to taste in a bowl. Whisk to combine, then add the oil, a drop at a time, and whisk until the mixture thickens, as when making mayonnaise. Continue adding the oil very slowly then, when it has all been incorporated, add the vinegar and dill. Alternatively, use the dill to garnish the fish. Taste for seasoning and turn into a sauceboat, bowl or jug.

To serve: scrape the spice mixture off the salmon with a sharp knife. Remove the skin by gripping the tail end with fingers dipped in salt and working the knife away from you between the skin and the flesh in a sawing action. Cut the flesh into 5 mm (¼ inch) thick slices across the width of the salmon. Arrange on a plate with lemon slices to garnish.

STEAK TARTARE

Trim any fat and membrane off the steak, then put the meat through the fine blade of a mincer (grinder) or food processor. Turn into a bowl and add the Worcestershire sauce and salt and pepper to taste. Divide the mixture into 10 equal portions. Form into rounds and make a slight hollow in the centre of each one.

To serve: arrange the steak patties on a large platter or tray and surround with small mounds of the diced and chopped vegetables and herbs. Beat the egg yolks together, then spoon a little into the hollow in each steak. Beat the mustard into the mayonnaise, add Tabasco and salt and pepper to taste, then transfer to a bowl.

Guests should help themselves to a portion of steak tartare, some vegetables and herbs and mustard mayonnaise, then mix everything together on their plates with a fork.

INGREDIENTS

900 g (2 lb) fillet (tenderloin) steak

1 tablespoon Worcestershire sauce

coarse sea salt

freshly ground black pepper

2 red peppers, cored, seeded and finely diced

2 green peppers, cored, seeded and finely diced

1 Spanish (yellow) onion, skinned and finely chopped

3 cooked beetroots (beets), skinned and finely diced

5 tablespoons capers, chopped

5 tablespoons finely chopped fresh parsley

5 egg yolks

2–3 tablespoons French mustard

450 ml (¾ pint/2 cups) thick home-made mayonnaise

Tabasco (hot pepper) sauce, to taste

CARPACCIO

Ask your butcher to slice the steak as thinly as possible, from the centre of a whole fillet. Aceto balsamico (balsamic vinegar) is available in bottles at Italian delicatessens; it is not expensive and will last indefinitely.

INGREDIENTS

6 paper-thin slices of fillet steak (filet mignon)

4 tablespoons Italian olive oil

2 teaspoons aceto balsamico

1 tablespoon very finely chopped fresh oregano or marjoram

300 ml (½ pint/1¼ cups) homemade mayonnaise, to serve

coarse sea salt

black peppercorns

Put a slice of steak between 2 sheets of dampened greaseproof (waxed) paper and bat out with a meat mallet or rolling pin until the meat is very, very thin – almost transparent.

Slice the steak into thin strips, roll up each one and thread on to cocktail sticks (toothpicks). Put the oil, aceto balsamico and oregano or marjoram in a bowl and whisk with a fork. Put the steak sticks in a shallow dish and drizzle over the dressing. Cover the dish and leave to marinate in the refrigerator overnight.

To serve: put the mayonnaise in a bowl and place in the centre of a platter. Arrange the sticks of steak around the bowl of mayonnaise, then grind a little salt and plenty of black pepper to taste over the meat. Allow to come to room temperature for about 30 minutes.

CEVICHE

Ceviche is a Mexican dish of raw fish marinated in lime juice. The acid juice whitens the fish so that it appears, and tastes, cooked. Don't be put off by raw fish – it is delicious.

INGREDIENTS

900 g (2 lb) monkfish or other firm fleshed white fish fillets

1 tablespoon coriander seeds

2 teaspoons salt

juice of 6 limes or lemons

1 bunch of spring onions (scallions), trimmed and diagonally sliced

185 g (6½ oz) can sweet red peppers, drained and thinly sliced

4 tomatoes, skinned, quartered and seeded, then cut into thin slivers

2 tablespoons chopped fresh coriander (cilantro)

½ teaspoon cayenne pepper

Remove any membrane and bone from the monkfish. Cut the fish into thin strips and place in a bowl. Crush the coriander seeds in a mortar and pestle, mix with the salt and lime or lemon juice, then pour over the fish. Turn the fish to coat in the marinade. Cover the bowl and leave to marinate in the refrigerator overnight.

To serve: remove the fish from the marinade with a slotted spoon. Drain the fish well, place in a serving dish and add the remaining ingredients. Fold gently to mix. Allow to come to room temperature for about 30 minutes, then taste for seasoning.

PUKKA PICNIC

*I*n days gone by, society lords and ladies picnicked in grand style in gazebos and pavilions, feasting themselves on whole joints and game birds, puddings and pies. Why not turn the clock back on this occasion, rediscover the pleasures of eating in the open air and return the picnic to its former glory? Be perfectly posh with crisply starched white linen spread out on the grass, white bone china, fine glasses, napkins, silver cutlery and cruet. For a proper picnic to be a success, it is essential to organize everything in advance, even enlisting one or two of your guests to help. All of the food on this bill of fare can be prepared ahead of time and is easy to transport – and nothing less than a wicker hamper will do. To be absolutely proper, get the men to wear blazers and bow ties, the ladies floppy hats and frilly frocks. And to add to the fun, open up the bubbly and make kir royale – a splash of crème de cassis in a flute of champagne.

SERVES 8

·

Picnic Terrine

·

Lamb Cutlets in Pastry

·

**Cheese and Courgette
(Zucchini) Rolls**

·

Tomato and Herb Quiche

·

Pan Bagna

·

**Apricot and Banana
Teabread**

·

PICNIC TERRINE

Stretch the bacon rashers with the flat of a knife blade and use to line a 900 g (2 lb) loaf tin. Work the belly pork in a food processor, then transfer to a bowl.

Work the chicken livers and bread in the food processor. Add to the pork with the Southern Comfort, peppercorns, sage and salt and pepper to taste. Mix well and bind with the beaten egg.

Put a third of the mixture in the lined tin and smooth the surface. Arrange half of the chicken slices on top, then cover with another third of the mixture. Repeat with the remaining chicken and liver mixture.

Cover the tin with foil, press down firmly, then stand the tin in a roasting pan. Pour in enough boiling water to come halfway up the sides of the loaf tin. Bake at 170°C (325°F) mark 3 for 2 hours. Lift the tin out of the water and leave the terrine to cool. Cover the terrine with fresh foil, place heavy weights on top and chill in the refrigerator overnight. Turn out the next day and wipe off excess fat with absorbent kitchen paper. Wrap tightly in foil to carry.

Contrary to what you might expect, terrines take no time at all to make if you have a food processor; they are also far less messy to make this way than in a mincer (grinder).

INGREDIENTS

12 streaky bacon rashers (bacon slices), rinds removed

450 g (1 lb) belly pork (fresh pork sides), rind and bones removed, cut into small pieces

225 g (½ lb) chicken livers

100 g (4 oz/2 cups) crustless fresh white bread

4 tablespoons Southern Comfort

2 tablespoons green peppercorns

2 teaspoons chopped fresh sage or 1 teaspoon dried

salt

freshly ground black pepper

1 egg, beaten

350 g (¾ lb) boneless chicken breast, skinned and thinly sliced

LAMB CUTLETS IN PASTRY

Cutlet frills, available from most good stationers and kitchenware shops, not only give an attractive finishing touch but they also help if you are eating the cutlets with your fingers.

INGREDIENTS

25 g (1 oz/¼ stick) butter

1 onion, skinned and chopped

25 g (1 oz/½ cup) fresh white breadcrumbs

2 tablespoons chopped fresh mint

squeeze of lemon juice

salt

freshly ground black pepper

2 eggs, beaten

12 lamb cutlets (rib chops), trimmed of fat

about 2 tablespoons groundnut or vegetable oil

two 368 g (13 oz) packets frozen puff pastry, thawed

Melt the butter in a heavy pan, add the onion and cook gently, stirring frequently, for about 5 minutes, until soft but not coloured. Remove from the heat, stir in the breadcrumbs, mint, lemon juice and salt and pepper to taste. Bind the mixture with half the beaten egg.

Brush the cutlets lightly with the oil and sprinkle with pepper to taste. Grill (broil) for 3 minutes on each side until browned on the outside but still pink in the centre. Leave to cool.

Roll out each piece of pastry on a lightly floured surface until 5 mm (¼ inch) thick. Cut each piece into 6 squares. Place a cutlet on each square so that the bone extends over the edge of the pastry. Reserve the pastry trimmings. Press an equal amount of stuffing on the 'eye' of each cutlet. Dampen the pastry edges, then wrap the pastry around each cutlet. Seal the edges well.

Put the cutlets on a dampened baking sheet with the seams underneath. Brush with beaten egg. Cut shapes from the pastry trimmings, place on top of the cutlets and brush with more egg. Bake at 220°C (425°F) mark 7 for 15–20 minutes, then reduce the oven temperature to 190°C (375°F) mark 5 and bake for a further 15 minutes until the pastry is golden. Leave until cold, then wrap in foil to carry.

CHEESE AND COURGETTE (ZUCCHINI) ROLLS

Put the grated courgette in a sieve placed over a bowl and sprinkle with the salt. Leave to dégorge for 30 minutes, turning the courgette occasionally to mix with the salt.

Meanwhile, sift the white flour into a warm large bowl and stir in the granary bread flour and yeast. Stir in the cheese, herbs and pepper to taste. Make a well in the centre. Press the grated courgette with the back of a spoon to extract as much liquid as possible. Add the courgette to the centre of the flour, then mix into the flour with a fork, gradually adding enough milk to bind the mixture together.

Turn the dough out on to a lightly floured surface and knead for 10 minutes according to yeast packet instructions. Return to the bowl, cover with a damp teatowel and leave to rise in a warm place for about 1 hour or until doubled in bulk.

Cut the dough into 8 equal pieces. Roll into balls, then place well apart on a lightly oiled baking sheet. Brush with melted butter, cover with lightly oiled polythene (plastic) and leave to prove for 30–45 minutes until well risen.

Uncover the rolls and sprinkle with the poppy seeds. Bake at 220°C (425°F) mark 7 for 15–20 minutes until golden (the rolls should sound hollow when tapped on the bottom). Cool on a wire rack, then wrap in foil or a plastic bag to carry.

These savoury rolls taste best on the day of baking. With easybake yeast they are quick and simple to make, but if you are still short of time on the day of the picnic the best solution is to make the rolls in advance and freeze them (they will keep beautifully fresh in the freezer for up to 1 month). Simply take them out of the freezer just before setting off on your picnic – they can be carried in their freezer wrapping.

INGREDIENTS

1 medium to large courgette (zucchini), weighing about 100 g (¼ lb), trimmed and grated
1 teaspoon salt
100 g (4 oz/1 cup) strong (unbleached all-purpose) white flour
100 g (4 oz/scant 1 cup) granary bread (whole wheat or graham) flour
1 sachet easybake yeast
50 g (2 oz/½ cup) grated Parmesan cheese
1–2 teaspoons chopped mixed fresh herbs or ½ teaspoon dried, according to taste
freshly ground black pepper
75–120 ml (3–4 fl oz/⅓–½ cup) milk, at blood heat
1–2 teaspoons melted butter
1 teaspoon poppy seeds

TOMATO AND HERB QUICHE

Most tomatoes benefit from being sweetened with a little sugar; however, in high summer you may find that the tomatoes are sweet enough and do not need any at all, or only just a pinch.

PASTRY

150 g (6 oz/1½ cups) plain (all-purpose) white flour

salt

75 g (3 oz/¾ stick) butter, diced

3 tablespoons grated Parmesan cheese

1 egg yolk, size 1 or 2 (large)

FILLING

25 g (1 oz/¼ stick) butter

1 tablespoon olive or groundnut oil

1 small onion, skinned and finely chopped

2 eggs, beaten

150 ml (¼ pint/⅔ cup) double (heavy) cream

2 tablespoons grated Parmesan cheese

2 teaspoons chopped fresh basil or 1 teaspoon dried

freshly ground black pepper

350 g (¾ lb) tomatoes, skinned and sliced

¼–½ teaspoon sugar

Make the pastry: sift the flour and a pinch of salt into a bowl, add the diced butter and rub in with the fingertips until the mixture resembles fine breadcrumbs. Stir in the Parmesan and egg yolk and mix to a firm dough, adding 1–2 tablespoons of ice-cold water if necessary.

Roll out the dough on a floured surface and use to line a 22.5 cm (9 inch) fluted flan tin with a removable base. Prick all over with a fork, then chill in the refrigerator for 30 minutes.

Meanwhile, prepare the filling: heat the butter with the oil in a small pan, add the onion and cook gently, stirring frequently, for about 5 minutes until soft but not coloured. Turn the onion into a bowl, add the eggs, cream, Parmesan, basil and salt and pepper to taste and stir well to mix.

Line the pastry with foil and fill with baking beans. Bake blind at 200°C (400°F) mark 6 for 10 minutes. Remove the foil and beans, return the pastry case to the oven and bake for a further 5 minutes.

Arrange the tomato slices in the pastry case and sprinkle with sugar. Slowly pour over the egg mixture. Bake for 20–25 minutes until the filling is just set. Leave to cool in the tin on a wire rack, then wrap in foil to carry.

*S*ucculent, tender lamb encased in
crisp, light puff pastry makes
Lamb Cutlets in Pastry
(page 60) the most perfect food for a proper picnic. To add an extra touch of
luxury, serve them with fresh asparagus encompassed in a ring of red pepper.
Follow with a crisp green salad to refresh the palate.

PAN BAGNA

INGREDIENTS

2 garlic cloves, skinned and roughly chopped

50 g (2 oz) can anchovies, drained and roughly chopped

8 tablespoons olive oil

8 'French bread' rolls

8 medium ripe tomatoes, skinned and sliced

two 190 g (7 oz) cans tuna fish, drained and flaked

185 g (6½ oz) can sweet red peppers, drained and thinly sliced

16 black olives, halved and stoned (pitted)

freshly ground black pepper

Pound the chopped garlic and anchovies in a mortar and pestle, then whisk in the oil to make a spreading consistency.

Cut each roll in half lengthways, leaving a 'hinge' so that the filling will not fall out easily. Scoop out some of the crumb. Spread the inside of the rolls with the anchovy and garlic mixture. Arrange the tomato slices on one half of each roll, then top with the tuna, sliced red peppers and olives, sprinkling each layer with black pepper to taste. Close the rolls up around the filling and wrap tightly to carry.

APRICOT AND BANANA TEABREAD

Bananas make this fruit and nut loaf beautifully moist. Although it is a difficult cake to resist, it is much better if left for at least 24 hours before cutting.

INGREDIENTS

275 g (10 oz/2½ cups) self-raising flour

2 teaspoons baking powder

½ teaspoon ground cinnamon

¼ teaspoon salt

225 g (8 oz/1⅓ cups) 'ready to eat' dried apricots, chopped

50 g (2 oz/½ cup) shelled walnuts, chopped

75 g (3 oz/6 tablespoons) caster (superfine) sugar

2 bananas

6 tablespoons milk

2 tablespoons groundnut or vegetable oil

1 egg, beaten

Grease a 900 g (2 lb) loaf tin, line with greaseproof (waxed) paper and grease the paper. Sift the flour, baking powder, cinnamon and salt into a bowl. Stir in the chopped apricots, walnuts and sugar.

Peel the bananas and mash in a separate bowl with the milk and oil. Beat in the egg, then stir into the sifted ingredients. Turn the mixture into the prepared tin. Bake at 180°C (350°F) mark 4 for 1¼ hours or until a skewer inserted in the centre comes out clean. Leave to cool in the tin for about 5 minutes, then turn out on to a wire rack, peel off the lining paper and cool completely. Wrap in foil and store in an airtight tin for at least 24 hours.

MEDITERRANEAN MEZE

*C*apture the magic of the Mediterranean with this mouth-watering Middle Eastern menu. In the Middle East, the sharing of food with family and friends is one of the greatest pleasures in life, and the informality of a meze meal lends itself beautifully to large scale entertaining. Arrange all the different dishes together on one large table and invite your friends to help themselves buffet style, sampling a little of each dish.

This menu offers a variety of exciting flavours and textures and each guest should try them all. Encourage guests to use their fingers to break off pieces of warm pitta bread then scoop up the food with the bread. Serve chilled retsina wine to drink and aniseed-flavoured ouzo spirit for those who have a taste for it, then refresh palates at the end of the meal with a selection of juicy ripe fruits such as figs, melon and grapes. Before your friends leave, offer them small cups of treacle-thick Arabic coffee, with cubes of sugar-coated Turkish delight.

SERVES 12–15

·

Avocado Cream

·

Hummus bi Tahina

·

Taramasalata

·

Aubergine (Eggplant) Caviar

·

Stuffed Vine (Grape) Leaves

·

Halloumi with Garlic and Mint

·

Tabbouleh

·

AVOCADO CREAM

Halve, stone (pit) and peel the avocados. Put the flesh in a blender or food processor. Reserving 2 tablespoons of the yogurt, add the remainder to the avocado with the rest of the ingredients and work to a purée. Taste for seasoning.

Turn the purée into a serving bowl and smooth the surface. Cover the bowl tightly and chill the avocado cream in the refrigerator until serving time.

To serve: uncover the dip, spoon the reserved yogurt on top and swirl with a palette knife (metal spatula).

Avocado flesh tends to discolour when exposed to air, but this dip keeps its colour extremely well. Once made, cover the serving bowl tightly with cling film (plastic wrap) and keep in the refrigerator. It should keep for a good 4–6 hours without turning colour.

INGREDIENTS

2 ripe avocados
150 ml (¼ pint/⅔ cup) Greek strained yogurt
150 ml (¼ pint/⅔ cup) homemade mayonnaise
juice of 1 lemon
2 ripe tomatoes, skinned and finely chopped
½ small onion, skinned and grated
2 garlic cloves, skinned and crushed
1 teaspoon paprika
1 teaspoon salt or to taste

HUMMUS BI TAHINA

For speed and convenience you can use canned chick peas, which need neither soaking nor cooking, and blend very quickly to a smooth purée. To make this quantity, you will need two 440 g (14.6 oz) cans. Dried chick peas vary enormously depending on how long they have been stored. If you use chick peas which have been stored for a long time, they will make a dry purée and you will need to thin the hummus down with more cooking liquid and/or lemon juice.

INGREDIENTS

225 g (8 oz/generous 1 cup) chick peas (garbanzo beans), soaked in cold water overnight

3 garlic cloves, skinned and roughly chopped

150 ml (¼ pint/⅔ cup) tahini

about 150 ml (¼ pint/⅔ cup) freshly squeezed lemon juice to taste

4 tablespoons Greek strained yogurt

2 tablespoons olive oil

salt

freshly ground black pepper

TO GARNISH

olive oil

paprika

chopped fresh parsley

Drain the chick peas and rinse well under cold running water. Put in a saucepan, cover with plenty of fresh cold water and bring to the boil. Drain, rinse under cold water to remove scum, then return to the pan and cover with plenty of fresh cold water again. Bring to the boil, half cover and simmer for 2 hours or until tender. Check the water level from time to time and add more boiling water so that the chick peas do not boil dry.

Drain the chick peas and reserve the cooking liquid. Set a few whole chick peas aside for the garnish, then work the remainder in a blender or food processor with 150 ml (¼ pint/⅔ cup) of the liquid and the garlic. Add the tahini and 100 ml (3½ fl oz/scant ½ cup) of the lemon juice and blend again until evenly mixed. Add the yogurt, olive oil and salt and pepper to taste. Blend again until smooth, then add more lemon juice and salt and pepper to taste. If the hummus is too thick, add more lemon juice according to taste and up to 150 ml (¼ pint/⅔ cup) more of the reserved cooking liquid.

Turn the purée into serving bowls and swirl the surface with a palette knife (metal spatula). Cover the bowls and chill in the refrigerator until serving time.

To serve: uncover the bowls and drizzle a little olive oil over the hummus. Arrange the reserved chick peas in the centre of each bowl and sprinkle with paprika and parsley.

TARAMASALATA

Crumble the bread into a bowl, pour over the milk and leave to soak for 10 minutes. Squeeze the bread with your fingers to extract the liquid, then put the bread in a blender or food processor.

Break up the cod's roe and add to the machine with the garlic. Work these ingredients until well mixed. Mix the oils together, gradually add to the machine, blending well after each addition until smooth. Blend in 75 ml (3 fl oz/scant ⅓ cup) lemon juice, then taste and add more lemon juice if liked. Blend in the hot water (this helps bind the mixture). Turn the taramasalata into a serving bowl and swirl the surface with a palette knife (metal spatula). Cover and chill in the refrigerator until serving time.

To serve: uncover the bowl and garnish the taramasalata with the olives.

This is a mild, creamy version of the immensely popular Greek smoked cod's roe dip.

INGREDIENTS

4 thick slices of white bread, crusts removed

6 tablespoons milk

100 g (¼ lb) smoked cod's roe, skinned

2 garlic cloves, skinned and crushed

150 ml (¼ pint/⅔ cup) olive oil

150 ml (¼ pint/⅔ cup) groundnut or vegetable oil

75–100 ml (3–3½ fl oz/⅓ cup) freshly squeezed lemon juice or to taste

2 tablespoons hot water

a few black olives, to garnish

AUBERGINE (EGGPLANT) CAVIAR

Put the aubergines on the rack of a grill pan and grill (broil) under moderate heat for 15–20 minutes, turning them constantly until the skin is black and blistered on all sides. Remove from the grill and leave until cool enough to handle. Carefully strip off the skin with your fingers.

Put the aubergine flesh in a blender or food processor with the garlic and work to a smooth purée. Add half of the tahini and lemon juice and blend until smooth, then blend in the remainder. Add the salt and a little pepper, taste and add more lemon juice and seasoning if liked. Turn the purée into a serving bowl and smooth the surface. Cover the bowl and chill in the refrigerator until serving time.

To serve: uncover the bowl and garnish the caviar with coriander and olives. Hand lemon wedges separately.

In the Middle East the aubergines for this dip are cooked on the barbecue rather than under the grill (broiler). Tahini is a paste made from sesame seeds and can be bought in jars from health food shops, Greek or Cypriot grocers or large supermarkets.

INGREDIENTS

2 large aubergines (eggplants)

3 garlic cloves, skinned and crushed

about 150 ml (¼ pint/⅔ cup) tahini

juice of 3 lemons or to taste

about ½ teaspoon salt

freshly ground black pepper

TO SERVE

coriander (cilantro) leaves

black olives

lemon wedges

STUFFED VINE (GRAPE) LEAVES

Cold *dolmas* or *dolmades* like these are traditionally made without meat, whereas the hot versions usually have minced lamb in the filling. This recipe is unusual in that it includes chick peas in the filling, which make it nutritious as well as very tasty.

INGREDIENTS

50 g (2 oz/scant ¼ cup) dried chick peas (garbanzo beans), soaked overnight in cold water

225 g (½ lb) packet vine (grape) leaves

200 ml (7 fl oz/⅞ cup) olive oil

1 medium onion, skinned and finely chopped

4 garlic cloves, skinned

2 ripe tomatoes, skinned and roughly chopped

50 g (2 oz/generous ⅓ cup) long grain rice

1 teaspoon ground cinnamon

½ teaspoon ground allspice

salt

freshly ground black pepper

3 tablespoons chopped fresh mint

50 g (2 oz/½ cup) pine nuts

juice of 2 lemons

1 teaspoon sugar

lemon slices, to garnish

Drain the chick peas and put in a saucepan with plenty of fresh cold water. Bring to the boil, then half cover with a lid and simmer for 1 hour.

Meanwhile, soak the vine leaves in water according to packet instructions. Heat 50 ml (2 fl oz/¼ cup) of the oil in a heavy pan, add the onion and cook gently, stirring frequently, for about 5 minutes until soft but not coloured. Crush 2 garlic cloves and add to the onion with the tomatoes, rice, cinnamon, allspice and salt and pepper to taste. Remove from the heat.

Drain the chick peas and chop roughly in a blender or food processor. Add to the rice mixture with the mint and pine nuts. Taste for seasoning.

Drain the vine leaves. Place one leaf, vein side uppermost, on a board. Put a heaped teaspoon of the filling at the base of the leaf, then roll up around the filling like a cigar, tucking in the sides as you roll. Do not roll too tightly or there will be no room for the rice to expand during cooking. Squeeze the leaf in your hand to seal in the filling. Repeat with the remaining filling and vine leaves to make about 30 parcels altogether.

Put the leftover ragged or torn vine leaves in the bottom of a large frying pan (skillet) or sauté pan (about 25.5 cm/10 inches in diameter). Arrange the filled leaves in a single layer on top. Cut the remaining garlic cloves into slivers and tuck between the vine leaves. Mix together the remaining olive oil, the lemon juice and sugar. Pour slowly into the pan. Cover with a lid and simmer for 1½ hours, pouring a little hot water in at the side of the pan from time to time as the liquid is absorbed. Remove from the heat and leave in a cold place overnight.

To serve: carefully remove the stuffed vine leaves from the pan and arrange in circles on a large round platter. Garnish with lemon slices.

HALLOUMI WITH GARLIC AND MINT

Put the block of cheese in a bowl, cover with cold water and leave to soak for 30 minutes. Drain, then pat dry with absorbent kitchen paper. Cut the cheese into pieces about 2.5 cm (1 inch) wide and 2 cm (¾ inch) thick. Spread out on a board and leave exposed to the air to dry for about 10 minutes.

Heat 1 tablespoon of the oil in a heavy frying pan (skillet) until smoking hot. Add 4–5 pieces of cheese and fry over high heat for 30 seconds on each side, just long enough to turn the cheese golden. Turn the cheese carefully with 2 palette knives (metal spatulas). Transfer to absorbent kitchen paper and leave to drain. Wipe the pan clean with kitchen paper, add another tablespoon of oil and heat until smoking hot. Fry the cheese as before and repeat until all the pieces are cooked, wiping the pan clean after each batch. Leave until cold.

To serve: arrange the cheese on a serving plate, cutting the pieces into thin slices if liked. Mix together the remaining oil, the lime or lemon juice, mint, garlic and paprika. Drizzle over the cheese and surround with lime or lemon wedges.

Halloumi cheese is available at Greek and Cypriot grocers and some large supermarkets. It can be very salty and is much loved in the Middle East where salty foods are popular, as in most hot climates. Soaking the cheese in water before using helps reduce excess saltiness. If convenient, cook the halloumi a day in advance and leave it to marinate in the oil and mint dressing in a cold place overnight.

INGREDIENTS

450 g (1 lb) halloumi cheese

about 150 ml (¼ pint/⅔ cup) olive oil

juice of 2 limes or lemons

2 tablespoons chopped fresh mint

2 garlic cloves, skinned and crushed

½ teaspoon paprika

lime or lemon wedges, to serve

TABBOULEH

Burghul is cracked wheat, available from health food shops as well as Middle Eastern delicatessens. It is whole wheat grain which has been boiled or soaked and baked until it cracks. Although time-consuming, the onions and herbs should be chopped with a knife; do not use a food processor as it bruises the ingredients, releasing pungent oils which make the tabbouleh taste unpleasantly bitter.

INGREDIENTS

225 g (½ lb) burghul

2 ripe tomatoes, skinned and finely chopped

4 spring onions (scallions), trimmed and finely chopped

25 g (1 oz/¾ cup) continental (flat-leaved) parsley, finely chopped

4 tablespoons chopped fresh mint

6 tablespoons olive oil

juice of 1½ lemons or to taste

¼–½ teaspoon sugar, according to taste

coarse sea salt

freshly ground black pepper

vine (grape) leaves or Cos (Romaine) lettuce leaves, to serve

Put the burghul in a large bowl, cover with 600 ml (1 pint/ 2½ cups) cold water and leave to soak for 30 minutes. Drain well in a sieve, then squeeze hard with your hands to extract as much moisture as possible. Spread out on a clean teatowel, cover with another teatowel and pat dry.

Tip the burghul into a large bowl, add the chopped ingredients, oil and lemon juice, with sugar and salt and pepper to taste. Mix well, then taste the tabbouleh and add more lemon juice and seasoning if liked.

To serve: line a large round serving plate with vine or lettuce leaves. Pile the tabbouleh in a cone shape in the centre.

*I*nvoke the sunny
flavours of the
Mediterranean with
(below, clockwise from left) Stuffed
Vine (Grape) Leaves (page 68);
Taramasalata (page 67); Tabbouleh
(page 70); Halloumi with Garlic
and Mint (page 69); Avocado
Cream (page 65); Hummus Bi
Tahina (page 66). Aubergine
(Eggplant) Caviar (page 67) is
pictured left.

AUTUMN

When the nights are drawing in, there is a real pleasure in inviting your friends round for a meal. If it's an Indian summer, then you can eat in the garden to savour the last of the sun, or throw an early evening barbecue around the bonfire to celebrate hallowe'en. Whatever the weather, if you choose one of the following menus the occasion is bound to be a success.

INDIAN SUMMER LUNCH

SERVES 8

·

Vegetable Samosas

·

Shami Kebabs

·

Vegetable Curry

·

Tandooori Chicken

·

Lamb Tikka

·

Gulab Jamun

·

Pistachio Ice Cream

·

Nothing could be more appropriate for a late summer lunch than Indian food. Everything can be prepared in advance – Indian dishes almost always benefit from being allowed to mellow and mature. The two main course dishes can be cooked outside on the barbecue, making it one of the most relaxed ways to entertain. Hand round platters of samosas and shami kebabs when guests arrive. They are dainty enough to be eaten with the fingers and plates are hardly necessary if you are eating in the garden. Guests can then choose between Lamb Tikka or Tandoori Chicken, which can be cooked on the barbecue fresh 'to order' and served with the Vegetable Curry.

Arrange the food to be cooked on a table next to the barbecue, then put everything else on a separate table some distance away so that the area around the fire is not too crowded. To give the table an Indian look, cover it in patterned raffia and make napkins out of inexpensive Madras cotton or paisley material. Indian breads such as chapattis, puris and naan on brass trays or baskets give an instant Indian look, so too do bowls of saffron-coloured rice and small bowls of accompaniments such as yogurt, cucumber, mango chutney, lime pickle, shredded coconut and rings of onion and banana.

VEGETABLE SAMOSAS

First make the filling: heat the ghee in a heavy pan, add the onion and cook gently, stirring frequently, for about 5 minutes until soft but not coloured. Add the potatoes, carrots, garlic and spices, mix well and fry gently for 10 minutes, stirring constantly.

Pour in 900 ml (1½ pints/3¾ cups) water, add the salt and stir well to mix. Bring to the boil and simmer uncovered for 15 minutes, stirring occasionally.

Meanwhile, divide the cauliflower florets into tiny sprigs and discard any long or tough stalks. Add to the pan with the peas and simmer for a further 10 minutes or until the vegetables have absorbed all the liquid and are tender. Remove from the heat, taste for seasoning and leave to cool.

Make the pastry: sift the flour and salt into a bowl. Work in the ghee with your fingertips, then add 100 ml (3½ fl oz/scant ½ cup) iced water a little at a time and continue working with your hands until a soft dough is formed. Knead for 10 minutes until smooth, cover with a damp teatowel and leave to rest for 15 minutes.

Divide the dough in half. Cover one half with the damp teatowel and set aside. Cut the uncovered half into 7 equal pieces. Cover these with another damp teatowel. Brush a little oil on a board or work surface. Roll out one piece of dough very thinly to a 10 cm (4 inch) circle and cut in half. Brush the edges of the semi-circle with water.

Place about 1 teaspoon of the cold filling in the centre, then fold one of the pointed ends of the semi-circle into the centre. Fold the opposite end into the centre, overlapping over the first so that a cone shape is formed. Brush the open edges again with water and press firmly together to seal. Cover with a damp teatowel. Prepare the remaining samosas in the same way.

Heat the oil in a deep-fat fryer to 190°C (375°F). Deep fry the samosas in batches for 2–3 minutes until golden on all sides. Remove with a slotted spoon and drain on absorbent kitchen paper while frying the remainder. To serve: arrange the samosas on a platter, with the yogurt, mint and chilli powder in separate bowls.

Samosas are usually served hot, but if you find it difficult to deep fry either just before or when your guests arrive, they can successfully be served cold. These vegetable samosas are just as delicious hot or cold, whereas meat-filled ones are definitely better hot. You can make the filling as chilli-hot as you like, but to suit individual tastes, both yogurt and chilli powder are offered as accompaniments.

FILLING

4 tablespoons ghee

1 medium onion, skinned and finely chopped

100 g (4 oz/⅔ cup) potatoes, scrubbed and finely diced

2 carrots, scrubbed and finely diced

2 garlic cloves, skinned and crushed

2 teaspoons garam masala

2 teaspoons ground coriander

1 teaspoon turmeric

½–1 teaspoon chilli powder, according to taste

1 teaspoon salt

100 g (4 oz/1 cup) cauliflower florets

50 g (2 oz/⅓ cup) frozen peas

PASTRY

225 g (8 oz/2 cups) plain (all-purpose) white flour

½ teaspoon salt

1½ tablespoons ghee, melted and cooled

groundnut or vegetable oil, for deep frying

TO SERVE

natural yogurt

chopped fresh mint

chilli powder

SHAMI KEBABS

The secret of making good shami kebabs lies in the quality of the meat. For the very best results, buy chuck steak, and ask the butcher to mince it for you, trimmed of all fat. Alternatively, you can mince it yourself or grind it very finely in a food processor. Some large supermarkets sell ready-prepared ground steak which has less than 8 per cent fat, and this would also be suitable.

INGREDIENTS

450 g (1 lb) lean chuck steak, minced (ground), or very lean ground steak

75 g (3 oz/scant ⅓ cup) split yellow peas (chana dall)

2 medium onions, skinned

8 pieces dried red chillies

25 g (1 oz/¼ cup) fresh root ginger, skinned and roughly chopped

2–3 garlic cloves, skinned and roughly chopped

1 cinnamon stick, broken into small pieces

12 black peppercorns

1–2 green chillies, seeded and finely chopped, according to taste

1–2 tablespoons chopped fresh coriander (cilantro), according to taste

1 teaspoon salt

1 egg, beaten

about 2 tablespoons ghee, groundnut or vegetable oil

Put the beef and split peas in a heavy saucepan. Roughly chop half of the onions. Add to the pan with the red chillies, ginger, garlic, cinnamon and peppercorns. Add 300 ml (½ pint/ 1¼ cups) water and cook over low heat for about 30 minutes, stirring frequently, until completely dry. Remove from the heat and leave to cool.

Work the mixture in a food processor, then turn into a bowl. Finely chop the remaining onion and mix into the ground mixture with the green chillies, coriander and salt. Bind with the beaten egg. Form the mixture into patties with your hands. Chill in the refrigerator for about 30 minutes.

Heat the ghee or oil in a heavy frying pan (skillet), add the patties in batches and fry over gentle heat for a few minutes on each side until golden brown. Drain on absorbent kitchen paper before serving.

*H*and round mouthwatering bite-sized Vegetable Samosas (page 73) while Tandoori Chicken (page 77) is sizzling away on the barbecue. Hot naan bread is one of the traditional accompaniments to Indian food; it can be made at home, but if you are pressed for time, buy it from a delicatessen or Indian restaurant.

VEGETABLE CURRY

The vegetables suggested here are intended only as a guide; others can be used if they are in season or preferred. Root vegetables are particularly successful in curries, so try to include at least one or two kinds, even in summertime.

INGREDIENTS

175 g (6 oz/2 cups) desiccated (shredded) coconut

½ cinnamon stick

1 tablespoon mustard seeds

1 teaspoon coriander seeds

1 teaspoon cumin seeds

1 teaspoon aniseed

2 tablespoons ghee, groundnut or vegetable oil

2 medium onions, skinned and roughly chopped

2.5 cm (1 inch) piece fresh root ginger, skinned and chopped

1 garlic clove, skinned and crushed

1 teaspoon turmeric

½–1 teaspoon chilli powder, according to taste

salt

150 ml (¼ pint/⅔ cup) natural yogurt

2 tablespoons tomato purée

450 g (1 lb) potatoes, peeled and diced

225 g (½ lb) carrots, scrubbed and sliced

225 g (½ lb) cauliflower florets, divided into small sprigs

225 g (8 oz/1½ cups) fresh or frozen peas

Put the coconut in a blender or food processor, pour in 300 ml (½ pint/1¼ cups) boiling water and work for 5 seconds. Turn into a sieve placed over a bowl and press with the back of a metal spoon to extract as much 'milk' as possible. Set aside. Retain 2 teaspoons of the coconut itself for serving.

Meanwhile, dry fry the cinnamon stick and spice seeds in a heavy frying pan (skillet) for about 5 minutes until they give off a spicy aroma. Grind in a mortar and pestle.

Heat the ghee or oil in a large heavy pan, add the onions and ginger and cook gently, stirrring frequently, for about 5 minutes until soft but not coloured. Add the garlic, dry-fried spices, turmeric, chilli powder and salt to taste. Stir well to mix. Mix the yogurt with the tomato purée and add to the pan a spoonful at a time, cooking between each addition until the yogurt is absorbed. Pour in 300 ml (½ pint/1¼ cups) cold water and bring to the boil, stirring. Add the potatoes and carrots, cover tightly and simmer for 30 minutes.

Stir the coconut 'milk' into the pan of vegetables. Add the cauliflower and peas, cover and continue cooking for 10 minutes or until the vegetables are tender.

Remove from the heat, leave to cool, then chill in the covered casserole in the refrigerator overnight.

To serve: reheat for about 10 minutes until bubbling well, adding a few spoonfuls of water if the sauce has thickened too much on standing. Taste for seasoning, then transfer to a warm bowl and sprinkle lightly with the coconut left from making the milk.

TANDOORI CHICKEN

Make the marinade: dry fry the garlic, ginger, coriander, mustard, cumin and cardamom seeds in a heavy frying pan (skillet) for about 5 minutes until they give off a spicy aroma. Grind in a mortar and pestle. Transfer to a blender or food processor, add the yogurt, chilli powder, salt and food colouring and blend well together.

Slash each chicken portion in several places with a sharp knife. Place in a single layer in a large roasting tin and pour over the marinade. Cover and leave to marinate in the refrigerator for 24 hours, turning the pieces over occasionally.

When ready to cook the next day, allow the chicken to come to room temperature for about 30 minutes. Arrange flesh side uppermost in the tin and pour over the ghee or butter. Roast at 200°C (400°F) mark 6 for 30 minutes. Remove from the oven, transfer the chicken pieces to a rack and place over the roasting tin. Sprinkle the chicken with half of the paprika and return to the oven for 15 minutes. Remove again, turn the chicken pieces over, sprinkle with the remaining paprika and baste well with the juices from the bottom of the tin. Roast for a further 15 minutes.

To serve: arrange the chicken pieces on a bed of shredded lettuce, onion and cucumber and spoon over a little of the juice. Garnish with lemon or lime wedges.

If you are using a barbecue, it is best to start cooking the chicken portions in a conventional oven for 45 minutes otherwise they will become too charred on the outside before they are cooked on the inside. Transfer them to the barbecue for the last 15 minutes before serving.

INGREDIENTS

8 chicken drumsticks, skinned

8 chicken thighs, skinned

50 ml (2 fl oz/¼ cup) melted ghee or butter

2 tablespoons paprika

MARINADE

2 garlic cloves, skinned and roughly chopped

2.5 cm (1 inch) piece of fresh root ginger, skinned and roughly chopped

1 tablespoon coriander seeds

1 tablespoon mustard seeds

1 tablespoon cumin seeds

seeds of 10 cardamom pods

250 ml (8 fl oz/1 cup) natural yogurt

1½ teaspoons chilli powder

1 teaspoon salt

½ teaspoon orange food colouring

TO SERVE

shredded lettuce

raw onion rings

cucumber slices

lemon or lime wedges

LAMB TIKKA

Shoulder and fillet are both quite fatty cuts of lamb, but they are chosen for this recipe because the fat is needed to keep the cubes of meat moist. If lean cuts such as leg and loin are used for cooking by dry heat, the meat will not be succulent and juicy.

INGREDIENTS

1.1 kg (2½ lb) boneless shoulder or fillet (tenderloin) of lamb, cut into 2 cm (¾ inch) cubes

lemon wedges, to serve

MARINADE

250 ml (8 fl oz/1 cup) natural yogurt

juice of 2 lemons

1 small onion, skinned and grated

2 garlic cloves, skinned and crushed

1 tablespoon vinegar

2 teaspoons aniseed

1 teaspoon chilli powder

1 teaspoon turmeric

1 teaspoon salt

¼ teaspoon orange food colouring

Put the cubes of lamb in a bowl. Mix the marinade ingredients together, pour over the lamb and stir well to mix. Cover and leave to marinate in the refrigerator for 24 hours, turning occasionally.

When ready to cook the next day, allow the lamb to come to room temperature for about 30 minutes. Thread the lamb cubes on to oiled metal kebab skewers. Cook under a preheated grill (broiler) or over a charcoal barbecue for about 20 minutes or until cooked to your liking, turning frequently.

To serve: transfer to a warm platter and squeeze lemon juice liberally all over.

GULAB JAMUN

This deep fried semolina dessert steeped in a scented syrup is unbelievably rich and sweet, so warn your guests not to serve themselves with too large a portion.

INGREDIENTS

100 g (4 oz/1 cup) ground almonds

100 g (4 oz/⅔ cup) semolina

175 g (6 oz/1½ cups) skimmed milk powder

50 g (2 oz/½ cup) self-raising flour

First make the syrup: put the sugar in a heavy saucepan, add 600 ml (1 pint/2½ cups) cold water, the cloves and cardamom pods. Heat gently until the sugar has dissolved, stirring occasionally. Bring to the boil and boil rapidly, without stirring, for 6 minutes. Remove from the heat and set aside.

Mix the dry ingredients together in a bowl, then gradually work in the yogurt, mixing with your hands until the ingredients combine. Divide into 24 pieces and roll into balls. Cover and chill in the refrigerator for 15 minutes.

Heat the oil in a deep-fat fryer to 190°C (375°F). Deep fry about

6 gulab jamun at a time for 2–3 minutes until rich brown on all sides. Remove with a slotted spoon and drain well on absorbent kitchen paper.

Stir the rose water into the sugar syrup. Carefully place the hot gulab jamun in a serving bowl and strain over the syrup. Leave to cool, then cover and chill in the refrigerator overnight.

To serve: uncover the bowl and sprinkle the gulab jamun with rose petals or pistachios.

2 teaspoons baking powder
about 150 ml (¼ pint/⅔ cup) natural yogurt
groundnut or vegetable oil, for deep frying
pink rose petals or pistachio nuts, to serve

SYRUP

225 g (8 oz/1 cup) granulated sugar
3 cloves
4 cardamom pods, bruised
1 teaspoon rose water or to taste

PISTACHIO ICE CREAM

Put the sugar, cornflour and 2 tablespoons of the milk in a bowl. Mix to a paste. Scald the remaining milk in a heavy saucepan. Remove from the heat and pour into the bowl, stirring constantly. Return to the heat and bring to the boil, stirring until thickened. Pour back into the bowl, stir in the condensed milk and leave to cool, stirring occasionally.

When the custard is cold, whip the cream until it just holds its shape. Fold into the custard with half of the pistachios and a few drops of food colouring.

Pour the mixture into a shallow freezer container and freeze for at least 4 hours until firm, removing from the freezer and whisking vigorously at least once every hour, to help break down the ice crystals.

To serve: transfer the container to the refrigerator for about 20 minutes to soften slightly, then scoop into glasses and sprinkle with the remaining chopped pistachios.

The texture of ice creams made in electric ice cream makers or churns is beautifully creamy and smooth because the mixture is kept constantly on the move. If you make ice creams regularly it is well worth investing in a machine – they are not expensive. This particular ice cream is out of this world when made in an electric machine.

INGREDIENTS

25 g (1 oz/2 tablespoons) caster (superfine) sugar
2 teaspoons cornflour (cornstarch)
450 ml (¾ pint/2 cups) milk
400 g (14 oz) can skimmed sweetened condensed milk
300 ml (½ pint/1¼ cups) double (heavy) cream
75 g (3 oz/¾ cup) unsalted pistachio nuts, skinned and finely chopped
green food colouring

LATE LATE BREAKFAST

SERVES 4
·

Champagne Cocktail
·

Salmon Kedgeree
·

**Mango and Passion Fruit
with Sabayon Sauce**
·

*T*ired with the dinner party routine? Then why not entertain Sunday brunchtime? Originally an idea from the States, a brunch party is intimate and informal, the perfect way for a group of close friends to get together and relax over good food and wine, especially on a cold autumn day.

Your brunch party should be a luxuriously lazy affair. Champagne and salmon, mangoes and passion fruit are such luxurious ingredients that the most discerning and sophisticated of guests can't fail to be impressed. Prepare as much as you can beforehand so that when friends arrive the food takes care of itself and the pace of the occasion can be as leisurely as possible. Serve large cups of fresh coffee to start, laced with a little liqueur if you like, the perfect pick me up for a Sunday morning. Then, when everyone's relaxed, wake them up with a special champagne cocktail, a sure way to liven things up. There's no need to sit round the table at brunchtime, a better and more informal idea is to set china, glasses and cutlery out on a low side table, in front of the fire if possible, then to pamper your guests by serving the food directly on to their plates. A little bit of luxury which everyone will appreciate.

CHAMPAGNE COCKTAIL

You can steep the sugar lumps in advance of serving for this cocktail, but do not open and pour the champagne until your guests are ready.

INGREDIENTS
4 sugar lumps
few drops of Angostura bitters
4 tablespoons Southern Comfort
4 tablespoons freshly squeezed orange juice
4 ice cubes
1 bottle champagne, well chilled
4 twists of orange zest

Put 1 sugar lump in the bottom of each of 4 champagne flutes. Sprinkle over the Angostura, then put 1 tablespoon each of Southern Comfort and orange juice into each glass.

Put 1 ice cube in each glass and top up with champagne. Serve immediately, with twists of orange zest to decorate.

SALMON KEDGEREE

Put the rice in a sieve and pick over to remove any stones. Rinse under cold running water until the water runs clear. Tip the rice into a bowl, cover with plenty of fresh cold water and leave to soak for 20 minutes.

Meanwhile, put the salmon in a frying pan (skillet), cutting it into two thin pieces if it is very thick. Pour over the wine and sherry. Slice 1 onion into rings and roughly chop 2 of the celery stalks. Add to the pan with the peppercorns, mace, cinnamon, bay leaf and 1 teaspoon salt. Bring slowly to the boil, turning the pieces of fish over once, then cover tightly with foil and a lid and remove from the heat. Leave to cool. Remove the fish from the liquid and flake the flesh, discarding the skin and any bones. Strain the liquid and reserve.

Finely chop the remaining onion. Slice the remaining celery into diagonal pieces about 5 mm (¼ inch) thick. Melt the butter with the oil in a large flameproof casserole, add the onion and cook gently for about 10 minutes, stirring frequently, until soft but not coloured.

Drain the rice and add to the casserole with the saffron, curry powder, half of the cayenne, 1 teaspoon salt and black pepper to taste. Stir over moderate heat for a further 5 minutes, then stir in the stock and the reserved fish liquid and bring to the boil. Lower the heat, cover tightly and simmer very gently for 15 minutes or until the rice is tender. Fold in the sliced celery for the last 5 minutes.

Gently fold in the flaked salmon and heat through. Taste for seasoning.

Although the most expensive rice you can buy, basmati is well worth the extra cost. Basmati rice is used extensively in Indian cookery, for its delicate flavour and long, slender grains. Most large supermarkets stock basmati, as do Indian grocers. The initial soaking is essential when cooking this type of rice, to remove excess starch and prevent the grains sticking together.

INGREDIENTS

450 g (1 lb) basmati rice

450 g (1 lb) fresh salmon

300 ml (½ pint/1¼ cups) dry white wine

4 tablespoons dry sherry

2 medium onions, skinned

6 celery stalks, trimmed

6 peppercorns, lightly crushed

1 blade of mace

1 cinnamon stick

1 bay leaf

salt

50 g (2 oz/½ stick) butter

1 tablespoon groundnut or vegetable oil

good pinch of saffron threads

2 teaspoons good-quality Madras curry powder

½ teaspoon cayenne pepper

freshly ground black pepper

900 ml (1½ pints/3¾ cups) fish stock

TO SERVE

4 hard-boiled (hard cooked) eggs, shelled

chopped fresh parsley

cayenne pepper

*T*he pretty garnish (left) on the Salmon Kedgeree (page 81) is simple to do. The whites and yolks of hard-boiled eggs are separated, then the whites are chopped, the yolks sieved. Above, the combination of Mango and Passion Fruit with Sabayon Sauce (page 84) and Champagne Cocktail (page 80) is stunning.

MANGO AND PASSION FRUIT WITH SABAYON SAUCE

If you have an electric whisk, it won't take more than a few minutes to whisk up the frothy sabayon sauce after you have cleared away the kedgeree. Prepare the fruit beforehand and everything will run smoothly.

INGREDIENTS

2 ripe mangoes
2 passion fruit
2 egg yolks
50 g (2 oz/¼ cup) caster (superfine) sugar
150 ml (¼ pint/⅔ cup) dry white wine
1 liqueur glass Southern Comfort

Peel and slice the mangoes and fan out on 4 individual plates. Cut the passion fruit in half and scoop the pulp and seeds over the mango. Cover and set aside.

Put the egg yolks and sugar in a bowl over a pan of gently simmering water. Whisk with a hand-held electric whisk, rotary beater or balloon whisk until the mixture is thick and mousse-like. Whisk in the wine a little at a time, then the Southern Comfort. Remove from the heat and continue whisking until cool.

To serve: uncover the fruit and pour the sabayon around it.

TEX-MEX MENU

SERVES 6–8

·

Empanadas

·

Tacos with Chilli

·

Crab Burritos

·

*T*reat your friends to a tex-mex meal. It's informal and fun, and an excellent way to pep up spirits at the onset of winter. Tex-mex food is a combination of Texan and Mexican, with a strong flavour. Fiery-hot chillies are an important ingredient in most dishes, so only invite friends who you know have a strong constitution! Tex-mex food looks most authentic in ethnic pottery bowls placed directly on wood. A scrubbed or bleached slatted table from the garden would be ideal, or you could cover a dining table with a Mexican rug or shawl if you have one. Cacti are the most suitable table decorations and a fun idea as a backdrop for the meal is to chalk up the menu in bright colours on a blackboard. Guests who like dressing up can go to town for a tex-mex party: the men can have long droopy moustaches, sombreros, ponchos and jeans tucked into their boots, and the ladies can wear full cotton skirts and petticoats in bright colours, with frilly off-the-shoulder blouses. Viva Maria cocktails are the ideal drink – shake together 4 measures tequila with 2 measures each lime juice and grenadine, 1 measure maraschino liqueur and 2 lightly whisked egg whites. Strain into cocktail glasses half filled with crushed ice and decorate with lime twists and maraschino cherries on sticks.

EMPANADAS

For the Mozzarella and onion filling: melt the butter in a heavy pan, add the onions and cook gently, stirring frequently, for about 5 minutes until soft but not coloured. Lower the heat and stir in the remaining ingredients with ½ teaspoon salt. Stir until melted and smooth. Cool before using.

For the spicy sweetcorn filling: melt the butter in a small heavy pan, add the onions and cook gently, stirring, for 1 minute. Stir in the flour, stock cube and paprika and mix well. Add the can of sweetcorn with its liquid and the tomato. Cook until thickened. Remove from the heat and stir in the cheese. Cool before using.

Make the dough for the empanadas: sift the flour, 2 teaspoons salt and the paprika into a bowl. Put the 2 tablespoons oil and the lard in a small pan, add 250 ml (8 fl oz/1 cup) water and heat gently until the lard has melted. Add to the flour mixture and mix with a fork to form a soft dough. Knead until smooth on a lightly floured surface, then wrap in cling film (plastic wrap) and leave to rest at room temperature for 30 minutes.

Roll out the dough on a lightly floured surface and cut into 10 cm (4 inch) rounds. Divide the filling between the rounds. Dampen the edges of the rounds and fold each in half. Press the edges to seal, then crimp.

Heat about 2.5 cm (1 inch) depth of oil in a frying pan (skillet). Fry the empanadas in batches for about 5 minutes, turning once, until evenly browned. Drain on absorbent kitchen paper. Arrange the empanadas on a warm serving dish. Serve warm.

Empanadas are very easy to make. This recipe gives a choice of two fillings – the quantity of dough given here is enough for one or the other. If you want to make both fillings, simply double the quantity of dough. Both the dough and the filling of your choice can be made on the morning of the party.

MOZZARELLA AND ONION FILLING

50 g (2 oz/½ stick) butter

2 onions, skinned and thinly sliced

225 g (½ lb) Mozzarella cheese, diced

1 egg, beaten

1 tablespoon chopped fresh parsley

salt

SPICY SWEETCORN FILLING

25 g (1 oz/¼ stick) butter

2 tablespoons chopped spring onions (scallions)

1 tablespoon plain (all-purpose) white flour

½ vegetable or chicken stock (bouillon) cube, crumbled

1 tablespoon paprika

200 g (7 oz) can sweetcorn kernels

1 tomato, skinned and roughly chopped

50 g (2 oz/½ cup) Cheddar cheese, grated

EMPANADAS

450 g (1 lb) plain (all-purpose) white flour

salt

1 teaspoon paprika

2 tablespoons groundnut or vegetable oil

100 g (4 oz/½ cup) lard (shortening)

extra groundnut or vegetable oil for frying

TACOS WITH CHILLI

Make the taco shells on the morning of the party, then reheat them for serving in the oven at 180°C (350°F) mark 4 for 5–10 minutes. Each guest fills a taco shell with some of the chilli, topping it with a choice of avocado cream, lettuce, soured cream or cheese. If you prefer to buy taco shells rather than make them yourself, they are available in boxes at most large supermarkets.

INGREDIENTS

3 tablespoons groundnut or vegetable oil

2 medium onions, skinned and finely chopped

2 garlic cloves, skinned and crushed

2 green chillies, seeded and finely chopped

3 teaspoons ground cumin

1½ teaspoons dried oregano

900 g (2 lb) minced (ground) beef

two 400 g (14 oz) cans chopped tomatoes

2 tablespoons tomato purée

salt

freshly ground black pepper

two 400 g (14 oz) cans red kidney beans, drained and rinsed

extra groundnut or vegetable oil, for deep frying

24 corn tortillas (as in Crab Burritos, see page 88)

TO SERVE

Avocado Cream (see page 65)

shredded lettuce

soured cream

coarsely grated mature Cheddar cheese

Heat the oil in a heavy saucepan, add the onions and cook gently, stirring frequently, for about 10 minutes until soft but not coloured. Add the garlic, chillies, cumin and oregano and cook, stirring, for a further 2 minutes.

Add the beef and fry until browned, stirring and pressing the meat well with a wooden spoon to remove all lumps. Add the tomatoes, tomato purée and salt and pepper to taste and stir well to mix. Bring to the boil, then lower the heat and simmer uncovered for 30 minutes or until the mixture is thick and quite dry, stirring frequently. Add the kidney beans for the last 5 minutes, to heat through.

Make the tacos: heat the oil in a deep-fat fryer to 185°C (360°F). Fold the tortillas in half and fry them 2 at a time in the hot oil until crisp, holding them against the side of the pan with a fish slice (pancake turner) or metal spoon to keep them folded over. Separate the tortillas and continue frying until golden. Drain on absorbent kitchen paper and keep hot while frying the remainder.

To serve: taste the chilli for seasoning, then turn into a warm bowl. Put the avocado cream, lettuce, soured cream and grated cheese in separate bowls. Arrange the hot tacos in a basket or on a tray.

*T*ex-mex food is fun to eat as everyone can help themselves. In the picture are two alternative fillings for the Tacos (page 86) – mushrooms fried with onion, green pepper, chillies and lime juice mixed with cream cheese, and shredded rare roast beef mixed with tomatoes, coriander, onions, chillies and lime juice.

CRAB BURRITOS

Masa harina is a yellow maize flour, available in some specialist delicatessens and food halls of large department stores. For best results, buy a tortilla press, available from kitchenware shops.

CORN TORTILLAS

225 g (8 oz/generous 1½ cups) maize flour (masa harina)

275 g (10 oz/2½ cups) plain (all-purpose) white flour

salt

SAUCE

2 tablespoons groundnut or vegetable oil

1 onion, skinned and finely chopped

two 425 g (15 oz) cans tomatoes

1 tablespoon tomato purée

1 tablespoon Worcestershire sauce

1 tablespoon paprika

¼ teaspoon cayenne pepper

FILLING

350 g (¾ lb) white crab meat, flaked

shredded lettuce

4 tomatoes, chopped

4 spring onions (scallions), finely chopped

100 g (¼ lb) Wensleydale or medium Cheddar cheese, crumbled

4 tablespoons soured cream, to serve

Make the tortillas: sift the flours and salt into a bowl. Gradually add 300 ml (½ pint/1¼ cups) warm water, mixing to make a soft dough. Add a little more water if necessary. Knead the dough on a lightly floured surface for about 5 minutes until smooth. Divide the dough into 24 pieces and roll out each piece to a 20 cm (8 inch) round. (The dough should be as thin as possible.) Place the rounds between sheets of waxed paper to stop them sticking while waiting to be cooked.

Heat a large heavy frying pan (skillet) (not non-stick) without fat. Add a tortilla and cook over moderate heat until just beginning to colour, then turn over and cook on the other side. As the tortillas cook, place them on a warm plate and cover with a teatowel.

Make the sauce: heat the oil in a heavy saucepan, add the onion and cook gently, stirring frequently, for about 5 minutes until soft but not coloured. Add the remaining ingredients with salt to taste and bring to the boil. Simmer uncovered for 20–25 minutes until pulpy.

Spread a little sauce over the centre of each tortilla. Sprinkle with crab meat, lettuce, tomatoes, spring onion and cheese. Roll up like a parcel, tucking in the sides to enclose the filling.

Place the parcels in a single layer in a buttered ovenproof dish and cover with foil. Bake at 180°C (350°F) mark 4 for 20 minutes.

To serve: pour the remaining hot sauce over the top with soured cream.

PINK PARTY

*O*ne of the simplest themes for a dinner party is to choose a colour so that food, drink, decor and dress blend together. Pink is one of the easiest colours to choose, as many ingredients are naturally pink and it is a flattering colour for decor and dress. There is a vast choice of table linen, china, glass and cutlery in pink, but try to keep these as subtle as possible so that the food is not dominated completely by them. Gold or silver creates a shimmering party atmosphere, especially by candlelight, and can be used to good effect to break up the pink. Silver or gold-plated cutlery, gold or silver-rimmed china, and glasses with a gold or silver trim are all widely available. A simple and inexpensive way to give a plain cloth a party look is to shake gold glitter over the tablecloth before setting the table.

Pink flowers are essential for the table centrepiece and a medley of roses and gypsophila give a pretty, old-fashioned air. You could also place a small posy of pastel pink flowers on each side plate, or simply scatter a few pink rose petals directly on to the cloth – this would give a romantic look. Offer guests kir (dry white wine with crème de cassis) as an aperitif, then move on to drink pink champagne or vin rosé.

SERVES 6

·

Prawn (Shrimp) and Smoked Salmon Charlottes

·

Fillet of Beef with Pink Peppercorn Sauce

·

Iced Raspberry Soufflé

·

PRAWN (SHRIMP) AND SMOKED SALMON CHARLOTTES

Line 6 lightly oiled 6×6 cm (2½×2½ inch) dariole moulds with smoked salmon, letting the slices overlap the edges slightly. Put the remaining smoked salmon in a blender or food processor with the cheese, prawns, 4 teaspoons of the lumpfish roe, the lime rind, paprika, salt and pepper. Blend until smooth.

Spoon the cheese mixture into the moulds, pressing it down well. Spread the surface evenly and fold over the ends of the salmon. Cover the moulds tightly and chill in the refrigerator overnight.

To serve: run a knife between the salmon and the moulds, then turn the charlottes out on to individual plates.

Pour the lime juice over each serving and garnish delicately with the unpeeled prawns and the remaining lumpfish roe.

Triangles of crisp, hot wholemeal or granary toast both look and taste good with these rich and creamy individual mousses, and a dry pink champagne complements their flavour well.

INGREDIENTS

275 g (10 oz) smoked salmon, thinly sliced
350 g (12 oz/1½ cups) curd cheese
225 g (8 oz/1⅓ cups) cooked peeled prawns (shrimp), defrosted and thoroughly dried if frozen
100 g (3½ oz) jar red lumpfish roe
finely grated rind and juice of 2 limes
1 teaspoon paprika
salt
freshly ground white pepper
unpeeled prawns (shrimps), to garnish

FILLET OF BEEF WITH PINK PEPPERCORN SAUCE

Pink peppercorns can be bought at specialist grocers and delicatessens, but if you prefer you can use red lumpfish roe instead, which looks equally good in this sauce. If using lumpfish roe, omit this from the garnish in the first course.

INGREDIENTS

1.4 kg (3 lb) piece fillet of beef (tenderloin)

2 garlic cloves, skinned and cut into thin slivers

freshly ground black pepper

2 tablespoons groundnut or vegetable oil

SAUCE

50 g (2 oz) pâté de foie gras

150 ml (¼ pint/⅔ cup) red or rosé wine

2 teaspoons redcurrant jelly

2 teaspoons pink peppercorns

150 ml (¼ pint/⅔ cup) double (heavy) cream

salt

about 100 g (4 oz/1 cup) fresh strawberries, sliced into fans, to garnish (optional)

Make small incisions in the beef with the point of a sharp knife and insert the garlic slivers. Tie the beef into shape with string, then sprinkle with black pepper to taste.

Heat the oil in a roasting tin, add the beef and fry over moderate to high heat to quickly brown and seal on all sides. Roast at 220°C (425°F) mark 7 for 10 minutes. Reduce the oven temperature to 190°C (375°F) mark 5 and roast for a further 25 minutes. Transfer the beef to a warm dish, cover loosely and leave to rest in a warm place.

Make the sauce: soften the pâté in a bowl by working in a few spoonfuls of the wine. Place the roasting tin on top of the cooker and pour in the remaining wine. Add the redcurrant jelly and bring to the boil, stirring and scraping up the sediment from the bottom of the tin.

Lower the heat, add the pâté and peppercorns and blend in well, then stir in the cream. Stir over gentle heat until well blended. Add salt and pepper to taste. Remove from the heat.

To serve: untie the meat and carve into neat slices. Reheat the sauce quickly, arrange slices of meat overlapping on warm dinner plates and drizzle over a little of the sauce. Garnish with fresh strawberry fans if liked. Hand any remaining sauce separately.

*P*ink food is
complemented by
gold table
decorations in this sophisticated
setting. Above, Prawn (Shrimp) and
Smoked Salmon Charlottes (page 89)
are garnished with prawns (shrimp)
and lumpfish roe; left, Fillet of Beef
with Pink Peppercorn Sauce (page
90) is served with radicchio and
walnuts.

ICED RASPBERRY SOUFFLE

Purée the raspberries in a blender or food processor, then work through a nylon sieve into a bowl.

Put the egg yolks, sugar and orange rind in a heatproof bowl standing over a saucepan of gently simmering water. Whisk with a hand-held electric whisk, rotary beater or balloon whisk until the mixture thickens and holds a ribbon trail. Remove the bowl from the heat and continue whisking until cool.

Gradually whisk in the raspberry purée and Southern Comfort. Whip the cream until it just holds its shape. Whisk the egg whites until standing in stiff peaks. Fold the cream into the mousse, then the egg whites. Add food colouring if liked. Pour the mixture into a wetted 900 ml (1½ pint/3¾ cup) soufflé dish. Cover and freeze overnight.

To serve: loosen around the top edge of the soufflé with a palette knife (metal spatula). Dip the base of the soufflé dish in a bowl of hot water for 30 seconds. Turn the soufflé out on to an inverted serving plate, decorate with fresh raspberries and orange shreds. Serve immediately.

To save time on the day of your party, make this soufflé in advance and store in the freezer. It will happily keep for up to a month.

INGREDIENTS

225 g (½ lb) raspberries, defrosted if frozen

3 eggs, separated

75 g (3 oz/6 tablespoons) caster (superfine) sugar

finely grated rind of 1 large orange

2–3 tablespoons Southern Comfort, according to taste

150 ml (¼ pint/⅔ cup) double (heavy) cream

few drops of pink food colouring (optional)

TO SERVE

fresh raspberries

blanched needle shreds of orange zest

TRICK OR TREAT SUPPER

*O*n a mild October evening, gather a host of friends together around the barbecue at twilight and treat yourselves to a warming hallowe'en supper. Witches, wizards and ghosts can come too, so long as they're appropriately dressed, carry jack o' lantern pumpkins and promise to behave! Light a bonfire for extra atmosphere and warmth, provide logs to sit on and light up the table with as many flickering candles as you dare – sinking them into tubs and buckets of sand as a safety precaution. Black is the magical colour for hallowe'en, with a touch of sparkling silver here and there. If possible, keep table, bowls, dishes and plates black, as the food in this menu is so colourful it will look wonderfully dramatic against a black background. If you don't want to buy a black cloth it's easy enough to dye a cotton sheet or use crêpe paper to cover a garden table. Paper plates and napkins are also available in black. And don't forget the apple-bobbing, the traditional game for October 31st. Float whole apples in a bowl of water, tie contestants' hands behind their backs and see how many of them can take a bite out of an apple without getting their faces wet.

SERVES 25

·

Skewered Potatoes

·

Sikh Kebabs

·

**Garlic and Herb
Grilled King Prawns (Jumbo
Shrimp)**

·

Vegetable Kebabs

·

**Cheese Wrapped in
Vine (Grape) Leaves
with Hot Herb Bread**

·

Liqueur Flamed Apples

·

SKEWERED POTATOES

Scrub the potatoes, then parboil them in salted water for 10–15 minutes until almost cooked.

Meanwhile, grill (broil) the bacon until very crisp. Drain well on absorbent kitchen paper. Chop the bacon roughly, then place in a blender or food processor and blend until very finely chopped. Add the paprika and oil and blend well.

Thread the potatoes on to lightly oiled large metal kebab skewers. Brush with the bacon mixture. Place on the grid of a preheated barbecue. Cook for 10 minutes, turning once.

The potatoes can be parboiled and the bacon dressing made on the afternoon of the party. Baste the potatoes with the bacon dressing as they cook on the barbecue.

INGREDIENTS
50 potatoes, total weight about 4.5 kg (10 lb)
salt
225 g (½ lb) streaky bacon rashers, (bacon slices), rinds removed
1 tablespoon paprika
300 ml (½ pint/1¼ cups) olive oil

SIKH KEBABS

Make the spiced lamb mixture the day before the party. Shape into sausages on the skewers in the morning, ready to cook on the barbecue in the evening.

INGREDIENTS

450 g (1 lb) onions, skinned and roughly chopped
4 garlic cloves, skinned
6–8 green chillies, trimmed and seeded if liked
15 g (½ oz/⅓ cup) fresh coriander (cilantro) leaves
1 tablespoon ground cumin
1 tablespoon ground coriander
1 tablespoon garam masala
2 teaspoons turmeric
2 teaspoons salt
2.5 kg (5 lb) finely minced (ground) lamb

Put the onions, garlic, chillies and coriander leaves in a blender or food processor and blend until finely minced (ground). Add the spices and salt and mix well.

Place the minced lamb in a large bowl and add the spice paste. Mix thoroughly with a large fork or your hands until well blended.

Shape the mixture into 15 cm (6 inch) long sausages on lightly oiled large metal kebab skewers. Place the skewers on the grid of a preheated barbecue. Cook for 10–12 minutes, turning frequently until evenly browned.

GARLIC AND HERB GRILLED KING PRAWNS (JUMBO SHRIMP)

Raw king prawns are available at high-class fishmongers. Oriental supermarkets sell these prawns frozen in packs.

INGREDIENTS

2.7 kg (6 lb) headless raw king prawns (jumbo shrimp)
4 garlic cloves, skinned and crushed
25 g (1 oz/¾ cup) fresh parsley, chopped
2 teaspoons capers, chopped
6 tablespoons lemon juice
150 ml (¼ pint/⅔ cup) olive oil
salt
freshly ground black pepper

Using a small sharp knife, cut down the outside of each prawn and remove the black intestine. Wash and pat dry with absorbent kitchen paper.

Work the garlic, parsley, capers and lemon juice in a food processor and blend in the oil until the mixture is slightly thickened. Add salt and pepper to taste. Pour over the prawns, cover and leave to marinate for at least 1 hour.

Drain the prawns and place on the grid of a preheated barbecue. Cook for 6–8 minutes until the flesh of the prawns is pinky white and firm.

*I*n the glow of the fire, serve Sikh
Kebabs (page 94) with Garlic
and Herb Grilled King Prawns
(Jumbo Shrimp) (page 94) and Skewered Potatoes (page 93). To drink, serve
The Bishop: heat together equal quantities of ruby port and water with sugar
cubes, clove-studded oranges and lemons and cinnamon sticks.

VEGETABLE KEBABS

Soaking the bamboo skewers in warm water prevents them from burning as the vegetable kebabs cook on the barbecue. The vegetables can be put to marinate several hours in advance of cooking. Bottled pesto (a sauce made from basil, pine nuts, olive oil and Parmesan cheese) is available at Italian delicatessens.

INGREDIENTS

450 g (1 lb) aubergines (eggplants)

salt

2 onions, skinned and quartered

900 g (2 lb) small courgettes (zucchini), trimmed

900 g (2 lb) red, green and yellow peppers

25 large bamboo skewers

MARINADE

450 ml (¾ pint/2 cups) olive oil

150 ml (¼ pint/⅔ cup) wine vinegar

2 tablespoons chopped fresh oregano or 2 teaspoons dried

1 tablespoon bottled or homemade pesto

freshly ground black pepper

Cut the aubergines into 2.5 cm (1 inch) cubes and place in a colander. Sprinkle with salt and place a plate over the top. Leave to dégorge for 30 minutes. Rinse under cold running water and pat dry with a clean teatowel.

Separate the onion layers. Cut the courgettes into 2.5 cm (1 inch) chunks. Halve the peppers lengthways, remove the cores and seeds and cut the flesh into 2.5 cm (1 inch) chunks.

Place all the vegetables in a large bowl. Mix together the ingredients for the marinade, adding salt and pepper to taste. Pour the marinade over the vegetables and stir to mix. Cover the bowl and leave to marinate for at least 1 hour, stirring occasionally.

When required, soak the bamboo skewers in warm water for 30 minutes. Drain, then thread with the vegetables. Place the skewers on the grid of a preheated barbecue. Cook for about 15 minutes, turning once, and brushing with the marinade.

CHEESE WRAPPED IN VINE (GRAPE) LEAVES WITH HOT HERB BREAD

Prepare the herb bread in the morning, ready to heat through in the evening. The cheese and vine leaf parcels can be prepared for cooking several hours ahead of time.

Soak the vine leaves according to packet instructions. Drain well. Cut the cheese into 25 or more 5 cm (2 inch) squares, about 1 cm (½ inch) thick. Wrap each piece of cheese in 1 or 2 vine leaves, depending on their size.

To prepare the bread, make diagonal cuts in the French sticks at 2.5 cm (1 inch) intervals almost to the base. Blend together the butter, garlic, spring onions and herbs and spread over the cut bread slices. Wrap the bread in foil. Bake at 200°C (400°F) mark 6 for 20 minutes until the butter has melted and the bread is hot.

Meanwhile, place the cheese and vine leaf parcels on the grid of a preheated barbecue. Cook for about 5 minutes until the cheese has softened. Serve with wedges of lemon.

INGREDIENTS

225 g (½ lb) packet vine (grape) leaves

900 g (2 lb) Gruyère cheese

3 large French sticks

225 g (8 oz/2 sticks) butter

2 garlic cloves, skinned and crushed

3 tablespoons chopped spring onions (scallions)

3 tablespoons chopped fresh parsley

2 tablespoons chopped fresh thyme

1 tablespoon chopped fresh tarragon

lemon wedges, to serve

LIQUEUR FLAMED APPLES

Core the apples and make a cut around the circumference of each with the point of a sharp knife. Place in roasting tins.

Beat the butter and sugar for about 5 minutes until softened. Beat in the egg yolks, then the cinnamon, ground and chopped almonds and almond essence. Fill the apple cavities with this mixture, pressing down well with a teaspoon handle.

Place 4 tablespoons water in each roasting tin and cover with foil. Bake at 190°C (375°F) mark 5 for 40–50 minutes until the apples are soft.

Warm the Southern Comfort in a small pan. Transfer the apples, with the cooking juices, to warm serving plates. Quickly pour the Southern Comfort over the apples and ignite. Serve immediately, with the cream handed separately.

This is a heavenly pudding, particularly appropriate for an autumn barbecue party, but also very good at any winter supper party.

INGREDIENTS

25 cooking (tart) apples

100 g (4 oz/1 stick) unsalted butter

100 g (4 oz/½ cup) demerara (brown granulated) sugar

2 egg yolks

1 teaspoon ground cinnamon

50 g (2 oz/½ cup) ground almonds

50 g (2 oz/½ cup) chopped almonds

few drops of almond essence (extract)

450 ml (¾ pint/2 cups) Southern Comfort

sweetened whipped cream, flavoured with vanilla essence (extract), to serve

WINTER

Celebrate winter in style. In the lead up to Christmas there's every excuse to throw a party – and the same goes for New Year. Whether you prefer a formal cocktail party, sophisticated soirée or just a fun evening gathered around the kitchen table with a handful of close friends, this chapter has something for everyone.

CHRISTMAS DRINKS PARTY

SERVES 30

·

Canapés

Saffron Stars

·

Red Pepper and Pumpernickel Crescents

·

Herb Butter Triangles

·

Cocktails

Margarita

·

Dry Martini

·

Tequila Sunrise

·

*W*hy not break with tradition this Christmas and go for sparkling silver, glass and black, a stunning combination for a Thirties style cocktail party? Thirties style dress will set the scene right from the start, and if you suggest this on the invitation guests will want to enter into the spirit of Deco decadence. Suave and sophisticated gentlemen of the Thirties wore dress shirts and dinner jackets for cocktails, while elegant and chic ladies wore silk, with feather boas and strings of beads. At any cocktail party, the drinks are obviously as important as the food. If you want to get everything right and enjoy yourself at the same time, the best solution is to hire a professional butler or barman, at least for the first couple of hours. This is a relatively inexpensive thing to do and worth every penny – the right person will not only mix the drinks but help hand round the trays of canapés as well.

To keep everything in style, look for Thirties cocktail glasses. Originals are collectors' items, but their modern equivalents are quite inexpensive. Deco shakers and swizzle-sticks are an essential part of the Thirties look, plus shimmering metal trays and coasters for serving. Shapes should be geometric and angular and vases of flowers can be used to co-ordinate the whole look. Black widow irises, lilies and orchids were favourite flowers in the Thirties and one or two blooms arranged in an appropriate vase are all that you need.

CANAPES

The following 3 types of canapé look and taste very different and yet are surprisingly simple to make.

SAFFRON STARS

Cut each slice of bread into 4 stars using a 5 cm (2 inch) cutter. Brush each star on both sides with melted butter and place on a baking sheet. Bake at 230°C (450°F) mark 8 for 5 minutes or until golden and crisp. Leave to cool on absorbent kitchen paper.

Meanwhile, blanch the yellow pepper halves in boiling water for 1 minute. Drain and rinse under cold running water. Leave to dry on absorbent kitchen paper.

Put the cheese in a bowl and add the curry powder, saffron water and salt and pepper to taste. Beat well to mix, adding enough milk to make a smooth, piping consistency. Spoon the mixture into a piping (pastry) bag fitted with a small star nozzle (tube) and pipe on top of the bread stars.

Cut out tiny star shapes from the yellow pepper using an aspic cutter. Place one on top of each canapé.

INGREDIENTS
1 large thin sliced white loaf
175 g (6 oz/1½ sticks) butter, melted
1 large yellow pepper, halved, cored and seeded
175 g (6 oz/¾ cup) full-fat soft cheese (cream cheese)
2 teaspoons curry powder
1 sachet saffron powder soaked in 1 teaspoon boiling water
salt
freshly ground white pepper
1–2 tablespoons milk

RED PEPPER AND PUMPERNICKEL CRESCENTS

INGREDIENTS

185 g (6½ oz) can sweet red peppers, drained

175 g (6 oz/¾ cup) full-fat soft cheese (cream cheese)

salt

freshly ground white pepper

1 red pepper, halved, cored and seeded

10 large slices of pumpernickel

Pat the canned red peppers as dry as possible with absorbent kitchen paper. Chop roughly, then place in a blender or food processor with the cheese and salt and pepper to taste. Work to a smooth purée.

Make hearts for the garnish with the fresh red pepper, as for the yellow stars in Saffron Stars (see page 99).

Cut 6 crescent shapes out of each slice of pumpernickel using a 5 cm (2 inch) plain biscuit (cookie) cutter. Spoon the cheese mixture into a piping (pastry) bag fitted with a small star nozzle (tube) and pipe on top of the crescents. Place one red pepper heart on top of each canapé.

HERB BUTTER TRIANGLES

INGREDIENTS

175 g (6 oz/1½ sticks) unsalted butter, at room temperature

12 tablespoons finely chopped mixed fresh herbs (eg parsley, thyme, marjoram, chervil, chives, basil)

juice of ½ lemon

1 teaspoon mustard powder

salt

freshly ground black pepper

1 large uncut granary (whole wheat) loaf

Beat the butter in a bowl with 2 tablespoons of the herbs, the lemon juice, mustard and salt and pepper to taste.

Cut all the crusts off the loaf to make a squared-off shape. Cut the loaf into thin slices, spreading each slice with herb butter before cutting. Dip the buttered side into the remaining chopped herbs, then cut each slice into 4 triangles.

COCKTAILS

The quantities given for the following 3 cocktails are for single drinks. To be correct, a cocktail shaker should be used to mix each Margarita individually, but when you are making a large number of cocktails this is impractical. Use a blender and mix several together at the same time.

MARGARITA

Put the egg white and salt on two separate saucers. Frost the glasses one at a time: dip the rims of upturned cocktail glasses first in the lightly beaten egg white, then into the salt. Keep each glass upside down over the saucer for a few seconds before inverting. Leave for at least 30 minutes before filling.

Put the rest of the ingredients in a shaker and shake until thoroughly mixed. Strain into the glass and serve immediately.

INGREDIENTS
1 egg white, lightly beaten
salt
50 ml (2 fl oz/¼ cup) tequila
2 teaspoons orange-flavoured liqueur
juice of ½ lime
crushed or cracked ice

DRY MARTINI

Put the vermouth in a chilled cocktail glass, add the gin and stir very briskly to mix. Pierce the olive with a wooden cocktail stick (toothpick) and place in the glass.

INGREDIENTS
1 tablespoon dry vermouth or to taste
50 ml (2 fl oz/¼ cup) gin
TO SERVE
1 stuffed olive

TEQUILA SUNRISE

Put the tequila in tall cocktail glasses, add the ice cubes and top up with the fresh orange juice, Stir, then slowly pour in the grenadine until it sinks to the bottom. Decorate the rims of the glasses with the lemon slices.

INGREDIENTS
50 ml (2 fl oz/¼ cup) tequila
ice cubes
100 ml (4 fl oz/½ cup) fresh orange juice
10 ml (2 teaspoons) grenadine
lemon slices, to decorate

*T*rays of Canapés (page 99) and Dry Martinis (page 101) look stunning in the Thirties setting (above) for a Christmas Drinks Party.

The colour co-ordination (right) is perfect in the Vegetable Terrine (page 106) and Red and Green Fruit Flan (page 107), two eye-catching dishes from the Red and Green Party.

RED AND GREEN PARTY

SERVES 10
·

Watercress Soup
·

**Avocado and
Red Pepper Ring**
·

Vegetable Terrine
·

Red and Green Fruit Flan
·

*A*n informal buffet with a colour theme is tremendous fun for the festive season. Red and green are the traditional Christmas colours, making it simple for you to co-ordinate your room with the food at this time of year. You will be spoilt for choice when it comes to decorations and tableware with a Christmas theme, but to give your party as tasteful a look as possible it is best to restrict your choice.

A theme of red satin bows looks cheerful and inviting and can be used throughout the house. A Christmas wreath of holly and ivy at the front door will welcome guests when they arrive and you can tie a red satin ribbon to it that will dangle down the door. Deck the hall and banisters (if you have them) with the same bows, then let the Christmas tree and table be the focal points of the room where guests are to eat. A Christmas tree looks quite dramatic simply tied with red satin bows, or you can use narrow red ribbon to tie home-made cookies on the tree Scandinavian style if you like. For the table centrepiece, set red candles in the centre of a holly and ivy Christmas wreath the same as the door and swag the tablecloth by pinning it with red satin bows. Buy a special Christmas tablecloth, or use a plain cloth and scatter contrasting glitter or sequins over it. Green or red on white looks Christmassy enough or you could go for a more dramatic effect with red on green or vice versa.

WATERCRESS SOUP

There is an abundance of fresh watercress around Christmastime to make this peppery-hot soup.

INGREDIENTS

50 g (2 oz/½ stick) butter
2 medium onions, skinned and chopped
4 bunches of watercress, trimmed and roughly chopped
25 g (1 oz/¼ cup) plain (all-purpose) white flour
900 ml (1½ pints/3¾ cups) vegetable stock
1.2 litres (2 pints/5 cups) milk
salt
freshly ground black pepper
2 tomatoes, skinned, quartered and seeded, to serve

Melt the butter in a large heavy saucepan, add the onions and cook gently, stirring frequently, for about 10 minutes until soft but not coloured. Stir in the watercress and coat in the butter and onion. Add the flour to the pan and cook for 2 minutes, stirring all the time.

Gradually blend in the stock, then the milk. Bring to the boil and add salt and pepper to taste. Cover and simmer for 5 minutes, stirring occasionally.

Purée the soup in batches in a blender or food processor until very smooth. Return to the rinsed-out pan and reheat. Taste for seasoning.

To serve: cut the tomato quarters into slivers. Transfer the soup to a warm tureen and float the tomato slivers on top.

AVOCADO AND RED PEPPER RING

Sprinkle the gelatine over the stock in a bowl and leave until spongy. Stand the bowl in a saucepan of hot water and heat gently until dissolved. Remove the bowl from the water.

Halve, stone (pit) and peel the avocados. Put in a food processor with the lemon juice and Worcestershire sauce.

Whip the cream until it just holds its shape. Stir the gelatine stock into the avocado mixture, then the mayonnaise. Fold in the cream and a few drops of food colouring. Taste and add seasoning if necesssary. Pour into a lightly oiled 1 litre (2 pint) ring mould, cover and chill in the refrigerator until set, for about 4 hours.

To serve: blanch the strips of red pepper in boiling water for 1 minute. Drain and refresh under cold running water, then pat dry with absorbent kitchen paper. Whisk the oil in a bowl with the lemon juice and salt and pepper to taste. Add the pepper strips and toss to coat in the dressing. Turn the avocado mousse out of the mould on to a serving plate and pile the red pepper strips in the centre. Garnish the edge with lettuce.

This mousse can be made up to 8 hours in advance, as long as it is not turned out of the mould until just before serving. It is very quick to make in a food processor and so can easily be made during the morning or afternoon before the party. When the avocado flesh is exposed to the air it tends to discolour, even when combined with other ingredients.

INGREDIENTS

1 tablespoon gelatine (unflavored gelatin)
150 ml (¼ pint/⅔ cup) vegetable stock
2 ripe avocados
juice of ½ lemon
2 teaspoons Worcestershire sauce
150 ml (¼ pint/⅔ cup) whipping cream
150 ml (¼ pint/⅔ cup) thick homemade mayonnaise
green food colouring
salt
freshly ground white pepper

TO SERVE

1 red pepper, cored, seeded and cut into strips
4 tablespoons groundnut or vegetable oil
juice of ½ lemon
shredded lettuce

VEGETABLE TERRINE

If you like, you can add a little green food colouring to the cheese mousse to keep strictly to the red and green theme. However, the creamy white of the cheese mousse helps set off the red and green vegetables beautifully, and a little cheating with the colours is allowed when the end result looks so stunning.

INGREDIENTS

about 30 young spinach leaves

275 g (10 oz) courgettes (zucchini), trimmed

two 185 g (6½ oz) cans sweet red peppers

salt

225 g (½ lb) French (green) beans, trimmed

juice of 1 lemon

1 tablespoon gelatine (unflavored gelatin)

450 g (1 lb) full-fat soft cheese (cream cheese)

dash of Tabasco (hot pepper) sauce, to taste

freshly ground white pepper

2 egg whites

Blanch the spinach leaves in boiling water for 10 seconds. Drain and rinse under cold running water, then pat dry. Use to line the bottom and sides of a lightly oiled 1.4 litre (2½ pint) loaf tin. Cut the courgettes into strips lengthways. Drain the red peppers, reserving the liquid. Cut the peppers into thin strips and dry very thoroughly with absorbent kitchen paper.

Bring 900 ml (1½ pints/3¾ cups) lightly salted water to the boil in a large saucepan. Add the French beans and blanch for 4 minutes or until barely tender. Remove with a slotted spoon, rinse under cold running water, drain thoroughly and set aside.

Add half of the lemon juice to the boiling water, then the courgette strips. Blanch for 3 minutes or until barely tender. Remove with a slotted spoon, rinse, drain and set aside as with the beans.

Add the reserved red pepper liquid to the pan of water, remove from the heat and measure 3 tablespoons into a small bowl. Sprinkle the gelatine over the liquid and leave until spongy. Stand the bowl in a saucepan of hot water and heat gently until the gelatine has dissolved.

Beat the cheese with 4 tablespoons of the blanching water. Add the remaining lemon juice with Tabasco and salt and pepper to taste. Beat well again.

In a separate bowl, whisk the egg whites until stiff. Stir the liquid gelatine into the cheese mixture, then fold in the egg whites until evenly incorporated.

Spoon a quarter of the cheese mousse in the bottom of the spinach-lined tin. Arrange the courgette strips lengthways on top. Follow with another quarter of cheese mousse, then the red pepper strips, arranging these lengthways. Repeat with more cheese mousse and a layer of French beans. Top with the last of the cheese mousse. Cover the tin and chill in the refrigerator overnight.

To serve: loosen the terrine from the tin by running a palette knife (metal spatula) around the edges, then turn out on to a serving plate.

RED AND GREEN FRUIT FLAN

Make the pastry: sift the flour and salt on to a cold work surface. Stir in the sugar and make a well in the centre. Put the diced butter and egg in the centre. With your fingertips, work the ingredients together to form a dough, adding 1–2 teaspoons very cold water to help bind together. Form into a ball, wrap in foil and chill in the refrigerator for 30 minutes.

Roll out the dough on a lightly floured surface and use to line a 25.5 cm (10 inch) fluted flan tin with a removable base. Prick all over with a fork then chill in the refrigerator for a further 30 minutes.

Line the pastry with foil and fill with baking beans. Bake blind at 200°C (400°F) mark 6 for 15 minutes. Remove the foil and beans, return the pastry case to the oven and bake for a further 10 minutes. Leave to cool, then remove the tin and place the flan on a serving plate.

Make the custard for the filling: put the egg, egg yolks, sugar and cornflour in a bowl and mix with 1–2 tablespoons of the cream. Bring the cream to just below boiling point in a pan, then stir slowly into the egg mixture. Return to the pan and simmer until thickened, stirring constantly. Remove from the heat, stir in the almonds, butter and 1 tablespoon of the Southern Comfort. Pour the custard into the pastry case. Cover with dampened greaseproof (waxed) paper and leave until the custard is cold.

Arrange the fruit on top of the custard in a decorative pattern, cutting the slices of kiwi fruit into halves or quarters if necessary. Warm the apricot jam with the remaining Southern Comfort, then boil until thick and syrupy. Sieve to remove lumps. Brush the glaze all over the fruit. Leave to set before serving.

The pastry for this attractive-looking flan is a very rich, French sweet shortcrust, call pâte brisée. It has a high proportion of butter and so is quite difficult to handle, but you will find the end result so crisp, light and delicious that your efforts will be well rewarded by the compliments of your guests.

PASTRY

200 g (7 oz/1¾ cups) plain (all-purpose) white flour
¼ teaspoon salt
3 tablespoons caster (superfine) sugar
150 g (5 oz/1¼ sticks) unsalted butter, chilled and diced
1 egg, beaten

FILLING AND TOPPING

1 egg
2 egg yolks
75 g (3 oz/6 tablespoons) caster (superfine) sugar
50 g (2 oz/½ cup) cornflour (cornstarch)
300 ml (½ pint/1¼ cups) whipping cream
50 g (2 oz/½ cup) ground almonds
25 g (1 oz/¼ stick) unsalted butter, at room temperature
5 tablespoons Southern Comfort
about 13 green grapes, halved and seeded
about 34 strawberries, hulled and halved
3 small kiwi fruit (Chinese gooseberries), peeled and sliced
175 g (6 oz/½ cup) apricot jam

NOUVELLE NEW YEAR

SERVES 2
·
Mange-tout (Snow Peas) with Cheese and Melon
·
Scallops in Ginger Sauce
·
Salad Leaves and Flowers in a Hazelnut Oil Dressing
·
Quenelles of Praline Ice Cream with Apricot Coulis
·

*A*n intimate dinner is the perfect setting to show off new-found culinary skills, and there is no better time to do this than on New Year's Eve, treating your partner to a taste of things to come …

Nouvelle cuisine calls for a fresh and innovative approach to food, so to a certain extent you can let your imagination run riot. There are no hard-and-fast rules, although ingredients must be of the highest quality and as fresh as possible. Cooking is kept to an absolute minimum in order to preserve natural freshness and goodness.

Presentation is all important, both for the food itself and for the table setting. Attention must be paid to every detail, so give yourself plenty of time, especially when arranging the food, garnishes and decorations on the plates. White is a favourite colour for tableware, simply because it enhances just about every kind of food, and glass too is a popular favourite, plain, patterned and coloured, especially for desserts and puddings. A pretty effect can be achieved by placing one plate on top of another, so that the food is framed as in a picture. This is extremely effective with glass on china.

MANGE-TOUT (SNOW PEAS) WITH CHEESE AND MELON

INGREDIENTS

12 even-sized mange-tout (snow peas), trimmed
salt
142 g (5 oz) packet garlic and herb full-fat soft cheese
4–6 tablespoons double (heavy) cream
finely grated rind and juice of 2 limes
freshly ground black pepper
1 Charentais (canteloupe) melon
2 tablespoons olive oil
1–2 tablespoons chopped fresh mint
fresh mint sprigs, to garnish

Plunge the mange-tout into boiling salted water, count 30 seconds, then drain into a sieve and immediately rinse under cold running water. Dry the mange-tout with absorbent kitchen paper. Slit along one side with the point of a sharp knife and gently ease the mange-tout open. Pat the insides dry.

Beat the cheese in a bowl with the cream, lime rind and salt and pepper to taste. Fill a piping (pastry) bag fitted with a medium or large nozzle (tube) with the cheese, then pipe into each mange-tout.

Cut the melon vertically into quarters, scoop out the seeds and remove the skin. Slice the flesh neatly.

To serve: whisk together the oil, lime juice, chopped mint and salt and pepper to taste. Arrange the mange-tout and melon slices alternately on individual plates, then spoon over the dressing. Garnish with mint sprigs.

SCALLOPS IN GINGER SAUCE

Detach the coral from the scallops. Slice the scallops in half horizontally, then pat dry with absorbent kitchen paper.

Melt the butter with the oil in a heavy frying pan (skillet), add the shallot and saffron threads and cook gently for about 5 minutes, stirring frequently, until soft but not browned. Pour in the wine and bring to the boil, then lower the heat and add the scallops, ginger and salt and pepper to taste. Simmer gently for 4 minutes. Add the corals and simmer for a further 1 minute.

To serve: with a slotted spoon, transfer the scallops to warm dinner plates. Increase the heat under the sauce, add the cream and whisk to combine. Taste for seasoning, then spoon around the scallops.

Dinner plates in the shape of scallop shells are available at many good china shops and department stores, and they would set this dish off well. If fresh scallops are unavailable, frozen scallops can be bought all year round.

INGREDIENTS

6 shelled (bay) scallops, defrosted if frozen

15 g (½ oz/1 tablespoon) butter

2 tablespoons walnut or hazelnut oil

1 shallot, skinned and very finely chopped

a good pinch of saffron threads

150 ml (¼ pint/⅔ cup) dry white wine

1 tablespoon finely chopped stem (preserved) ginger

salt

freshly ground white pepper

2 tablespoons double (heavy) cream

*B*ouquets of fresh vegetables (left)
give a nouvelle cuisine look to
Scallops in Ginger Sauce
(page 109). The beans are tied with a carrot ribbon and carrots with a single
chive. A serving of Quenelles of Praline Ice Cream with Apricot Coulis
(page 113) is daintily displayed on double plates (above), with crisp rolled
wafers served separately.

SALAD LEAVES AND FLOWERS IN A HAZELNUT OIL DRESSING

Edible nasturtiums are available in many large supermarkets and specialist greengrocers. In the late summer and early autumn they grow prolifically in the garden and are well worth cultivating for use in salads, and as a garnish or decoration for both sweet and savoury dishes.

INGREDIENTS

¼ oak leaf or batavia lettuce, washed and separated into leaves

4 radicchio (red lettuce) leaves

a few nasturtium leaves

2 tablespoons finely chopped mixed fresh herbs (including tarragon)

DRESSING

4 tablespoons hazelnut oil

1 tablespoon lemon juice

½ teaspoon tarragon mustard

salt

freshly ground black pepper

TO SERVE

2 tablespoons coarsely chopped hazelnuts

a few nasturtium flowers

First make the dressing: put the oil and lemon juice in a large bowl with the mustard and salt and pepper to taste. Whisk with a fork until thickened.

Tear the lettuce, radicchio and nasturtium leaves into the bowl. Add the herbs and toss gently until the leaves are coated in the dressing.

To serve: transfer the salad to a serving bowl and sprinkle over the hazelnuts. Arrange the nasturtium flowers amongst the salad leaves.

QUENELLES OF PRALINE ICE CREAM WITH APRICOT COULIS

Make the praline: have ready a lightly oiled shallow cake tin. A Swiss roll tin (jelly roll pan) is ideal. Put the almonds and 75 g (3 oz/6 tablespoons) of the sugar in a heavy saucepan. Heat gently until the sugar melts and caramelizes to a rich golden brown. Turn into the oiled tin and leave until cold and set. Break up with a rolling pin, then crush to a fine powder in a nut mill or food processor.

Put the egg yolks in a bowl over a pan of gently simmering water. Put the remaining sugar in a clean heavy saucepan. Add 120 ml (4 fl oz/scant ⅓ cup) cold water and heat gently until the sugar has dissolved. Increase the heat and boil for 3–5 minutes, without stirring, until a light syrup is formed. Remove from the heat and whisk into the egg yolks with an electric whisk until thick. Remove the bowl from the heat and whisk until cold. Stir in the cream, vanilla essence and praline. Stiffly whisk the egg whites and fold into the mixture until evenly incorporated. Pour into a shallow freezer container and freeze for about 2 hours until ice crystals form about 2.5 cm (1 inch) in from the edge. Beat with a fork, then cover and freeze overnight.

Make the apricot coulis: put the apricots in a heavy pan with just enough water to cover the bottom. Cover and poach until soft. Push the flesh through a nylon sieve into a bowl. Stir in the Southern Comfort and sugar to taste. Cover the bowl and chill in the refrigerator overnight.

To serve: transfer the ice cream to the refrigerator to soften for 30 minutes. Shape into 6 quenelles with dessertspoons. Arrange 3 quenelles on each individual plate and return to the freezer. When ready to serve, remove the plates from the freezer and flood with the chilled apricot coulis.

An electric ice cream maker or churn greatly improves the texture of this ice, as it does the Pistachio Ice Cream on page 79, making it smooth and velvety in texture.

INGREDIENTS

75 g (3 oz/¾ cup) unblanched almonds

115 g (4½ oz/⅔ cup) caster (superfine) sugar

3 eggs, separated, size 1 or 2 (large)

300 ml (½ pint/1¼ cups) whipping cream

½ teaspoon vanilla essence (extract)

APRICOT COULIS

225 g (½ lb) fresh apricots, halved

2 tablespoons Southern Comfort

caster (superfine) sugar, to taste

SHANGHAI STIR FRY

SERVES 4
·

Stir Fried Steak with Mango
·

**Prawns (Shrimp)
with Waterchestnuts and
Mange-tout (Snow Peas)**
·

Baked Whole Sea Bass
·

**Shredded Carrots
with Beansprouts, Ginger
and Orange**
·

*T*he art of stir frying is fascinating to watch, yet simple and fun to do. One of the best ways to hold a party with a Chinese theme is to invite friends into the kitchen so that everything is at hand for last-minute cooking and they can be entertained by the spectacle at the stove! Organization is the keynote of success. Absolutely everything must be prepared and ready for cooking before guests arrive, laid out in neat tidy rows so that one by one ingredients can be literally whisked into the wok. These will look so attractive when guests assemble in the kitchen that there will be no need for further decorations.

Black and white are often used for oriental table settings as they set off the brilliant colours of individual ingredients so beautifully. The whole sea bass makes a spectacular enough centrepiece for this table, then at each place setting a white Chinese bowl placed on a black under plate will make an immediate impact, together with black chopsticks placed on white chopstick rests. At each place setting, float a white chrysanthemum in a shallow bowl, and instead of napkins give the table an oriental touch with black or white damp flannels. Soak them in jasmine-scented boiling hot water, then wring them out until damp but still hot.

STIR FRIED STEAK WITH MANGO

INGREDIENTS

350 g (¾ lb) rump steak, trimmed of fat and cut into 5×2.5 cm (2×1 inch) strips
2 tablespoons groundnut or vegetable oil
2 small green chillies, finely chopped
1 garlic clove, skinned and crushed
1 bunch of spring onions (scallions), trimmed and diagonally sliced
1 small green pepper, cored, seeded and shredded
1 ripe mango, peeled and cut into thin slices
1 tablespoon soy sauce
1 tablespoon dry sherry
salt

Put the steak in a bowl with 1 tablespoon of the oil, the chillies (seeded if preferred) and garlic. Mix well and leave to stand for about 10 minutes.

Heat the remaining oil in a preheated wok or deep heavy frying pan (skillet), add the steak and stir fry for 2 minutes. Add the spring onions and green pepper and stir fry for 1 minute, then stir in the mango, soy sauce, sherry and salt to taste. Heat through, stirring gently so that the mango does not break up.

Prawns (Shrimp) with Water Chestnuts and Mange-Tout (Snow Peas) (page 116) pictured here is just one of the three colourful stir-fries in this informal supper menu for four. All three dishes look good on the table arranged around the spectacular centrepiece of Baked Whole Sea Bass (page 116). Boiled rice is the only accompaniment necessary.

PRAWNS (SHRIMP) WITH WATERCHESTNUTS AND MANGE-TOUT (SNOW PEAS)

INGREDIENTS

2 tablespoons groundnut or vegetable oil

225 g (½ lb) mange-tout (snow peas), trimmed

1 garlic clove, skinned and crushed

450 g (1 lb) prawns (shrimp), defrosted if frozen

230 g (8 oz) can waterchestnuts, drained and sliced

2 tablespoons sesame seeds, toasted

2 tablespoons soy sauce

salt

freshly ground black pepper

1 tablespoon sesame seed oil

Heat the oil in a preheated wok or deep heavy frying pan (skillet), add the mange-tout and garlic and stir fry for 2 minutes. Add the prawns and stir fry for 1 minute. Stir in the remaining ingredients, except the sesame oil, with salt and pepper to taste. Stir fry for 2 minutes to heat through, tossing the pan to combine the ingredients evenly. Sprinkle over the sesame oil just before serving.

Note: If liked, stir in 2 tablespoons bottled chilli sauce.

BAKED WHOLE SEA BASS

This simple fish dish can be prepared up to the baking stage the night before. In fact, overnight marinating in the refrigerator will improve the flavour.

INGREDIENTS

900 g (2 lb) whole sea bass, gutted, with head and tail left on

1 bunch of spring onions (scallions), trimmed

5 cm (2 inch) piece fresh root ginger, skinned and cut into matchstick strips

2 tablespoons sake (rice wine) or dry sherry

2 tablespoons soy sauce

1 teaspoon caster (superfine) sugar

salt

freshly ground black pepper

spring onion (scallion) tassels, to garnish

Wash the fish inside and out, then pat dry with absorbent kitchen paper. Make diagonal slits on each side of the fish with a sharp knife. Place half of the spring onions on a large sheet of lightly oiled foil and place the fish on top of them. Put the remaining spring onions inside the fish, with the strips of ginger.

Mix together the sake or sherry, soy sauce, sugar and salt and pepper to taste. Pour this mixture over the fish, then wrap in the foil. Leave to stand for at least 30 minutes.

Place the foil-wrapped fish in a lightly oiled baking dish. Bake at 180°C (350°F) mark 4 for 20 minutes.

To serve: carefully unwrap the fish and lift off the foil with 2 fish slices (pancake turners) on to a warm platter. Garnish with spring onion tassels.

SHREDDED CARROTS WITH BEANSPROUTS, GINGER AND ORANGE

Pare 3–4 strips of zest from 1 orange, blanch in boiling water for 1 minute, then drain and refresh under cold running water. Pat dry with absorbent kitchen paper and cut into thin shreds. Remove the remaining zest and the pith from the orange and discard. Cut the orange into segments. Squeeze the juice from the remaining orange.

Put the carrots and ginger in a bowl, stir in 2 tablespoons of the oil and leave to stand for about 10 minutes. Stir in the orange and lemon juice with the Southern Comfort or sherry.

Heat the remaining oil in a preheated wok or deep heavy frying pan (skillet), add the carrots and ginger mixture and stir fry for 3 minutes. Add the beansprouts and stir fry for a further 2 minutes, then stir in the remaining ingredients with salt and pepper to taste. Stir fry to heat through, tossing the pan to combine the ingredients evenly.

Fresh, light and fruity, this vegetable stir fry provides a pleasing contrast to the other, more flavoursome Chinese-style dishes in this menu.

INGREDIENTS

2 oranges
350 g (¾ lb) carrots, scrubbed and cut into matchstick strips
25 g (1 oz) fresh root ginger, skinned and cut into matchstick strips
4 tablespoons groundnut or vegetable oil
2 tablespoons lemon juice
2 tablespoons Southern Comfort or sherry
350 g (¾ lb) beansprouts
salt
freshly ground black pepper

DINNER A DEUX

SERVES 2
·

Salade Tiède
·

Paupiettes de Sole
·

Coeurs à la Crème
·

*S*et a round table intimately for two, light the candles and celebrate St. Valentine's Day in style with your loved one. A theme of hearts runs through the three different courses in this romantically inspired menu, so why not carry the romantic touch through to the table setting? Red roses are a symbol of love, and a pretty posy of roses and gypsophila would be the perfect table centrepiece. If you prefer a more subtle arrangement, then simply place a single red or pink rosebud across the napkin on each side plate and entwine the stem of the rose with goldheart ivy. Or be thoroughly sentimental and old-fashioned and make special place cards with a hearts and flowers theme as the Victorians did. Pretty paper doileys, pink tissue and ribbon can be used to create romantic cards, and if you decorate them with Victorian love message stickers they make beautiful keepsakes, fitting reminders for such a memorable meal.

SALADE TIEDE

Many supermarkets sell ready-prepared packs of continental-style salad which include a mixture of seasonal salad leaves such as those listed below.

INGREDIENTS

4 tablespoons walnut or hazelnut oil

100 g (¼ lb) chicken livers, defrosted if frozen, sliced

25–50 g (1–2 oz) lamb's lettuce

1 head chicory (endive), separated into leaves

¼ head curly endive (chicory), separated

few radicchio (red lettuce) leaves

2 tablespoons chopped mixed fresh herbs

3 tablespoons raspberry vinegar

salt

freshly ground black pepper

CROUTONS

3 slices of stale white bread, crusts removed

2–3 tablespoons walnut or hazelnut oil

First make the croûtons: stamp heart shapes out of the bread using a small cutter. Heat the oil in a heavy frying pan (skillet), add the heart shapes and fry over moderate heat until golden on both sides. Remove with a slotted spoon and keep warm on absorbent kitchen paper. Wipe the frying pan clean.

Heat 1 tablespoon of the oil in the frying pan, add the slices of chicken livers and toss over high heat for 3–5 minutes, according to the thickness of the livers. The centres should still be pink or the liver will be tough. Remove the livers with a slotted spoon and keep warm.

Toss the salad leaves and herbs together in a large bowl. Add the vinegar to the frying pan and boil to reduce, stirring vigorously to scrape up the sediment from the chicken livers. Add the remaining oil and stir well until heated through, then pour over the salad.

To serve: add the chicken livers to the salad with salt and pepper to taste. Toss lightly to mix. Garnish with the croûtons.

*H*earts form the central theme of this romantically inspired menu for two. Below, the main course of *Paupiettes de Sole* (page 120) is garnished with tiny hearts made from cucumber skin. Left, the *Coeurs à la Crème* for dessert (page 121) are set in heart-shaped moulds.

PAUPIETTES DE SOLE

The stuffing and sauce for these paupiettes is similar in flavour to Taramasalata (page 67); its strong 'fishy' flavour complements the delicate sole. Salt is not included because of the saltiness of the smoked cod's roe. To make cucumber 'hearts', peel off the skin from ½ cucumber, then stamp out hearts from the skin with a heart-shaped aspic cutter.

INGREDIENTS

1 lemon sole, weighing 550–700 g (1¼–1½ lb), skinned and filleted, bones and skin reserved

1 bouquet garni

1 small onion, skinned and sliced

1 celery stalk, trimmed and halved

1 carrot, scraped and roughly chopped

6 black peppercorns

75 g (3 oz) smoked cod's roe, skinned

2 teaspoons onion juice

2 teaspoons lemon juice

4 tablespoons fresh wholemeal (whole wheat) breadcrumbs

150 ml (¼ pint/⅔ cup) double (heavy) or whipping cream

freshly ground white pepper

1 egg yolk

cucumber 'hearts', to garnish

Make the fish stock: put the bones and skin from the sole in a saucepan, add the bouquet garni, onion, celery, carrot and peppercorns and cover with cold water. Bring to the boil, cover and simmer for 20 minutes. Strain into a measuring jug.

Trim and cut the sole to make 4 'quarter' fillets. Place skinned side up on a board.

Make the stuffing: put the cod's roe in a bowl and mash well with a fork. Blend in the onion and lemon juice. Put a third of this mixture into a separate heatproof bowl and set aside for the sauce. Add the breadcrumbs and 1 tablespoon of the cream to the bowl of stuffing, with pepper to taste. Beat well to mix. Divide the stuffing into 4 and place one portion at the thick end of each sole fillet. Spread halfway along the fillets, then roll up towards the narrow part.

Bring 120 ml (4 fl oz/½ cup) of the fish stock to the boil in a wide saucepan. Lower the heat, add the paupiettes, cover and poach gently for 15 minutes.

Meanwhile, add the remaining cream and the egg yolk to the reserved cod's roe mixture, with pepper to taste. Beat well to mix. Place the bowl over a pan of gently simmering water and stir until the sauce coats the back of the spoon. Remove from the heat.

To serve: flood 2 warm dinner plates with the sauce. Place 2 paupiettes on each plate and garnish with cucumber hearts. Serve with buttered courgettes.

COEURS A LA CREME

Press the cottage cheese through a nylon sieve into a bowl. Add the sugar and beat well to mix.

Whip the cream with the lemon juice until it holds its shape. In a separate bowl, whisk the egg white until stiff. Stir the cream into the cheese mixture, then fold in the egg white. Press the mixture into 2 individual heart-shaped moulds, place them on saucers and leave to drain in the refrigerator overnight.

To serve: put the strawberries in a bowl, sliced if liked, then pour over the Southern Comfort. Leave to stand at room temperature for 20–30 minutes, stirring occasionally. Serve the coeurs à la crème and strawberries separately.

If you prefer to turn these hearts out for serving, the moulds will have to be lined with muslin or cheesecloth before pressing in the cheese mixture.

INGREDIENTS

100 g (4 oz/½ cup) cottage cheese

15 g (½ oz/1 tablespoon) caster (superfine) sugar

150 ml (¼ pint/⅔ cup) double (heavy) cream

½ teaspoon lemon juice

1 egg white

225 g/1 punnet (about ½ lb) fresh strawberries, hulled

2–3 tablespoons Southern Comfort

BLACK AND WHITE SOIREE

SERVES 10–15

·

Gorgonzola Prunes

·

Blini

·

Black Grape Cheesecake

·

*E*legance is the theme of this sophisticated soirée. Black and white together make incredible impact and your party should be nothing less than a really stunning affair. It's simple to create an up-to-the-minute high-tech look with the dramatic combination of black and white, plus a splash of red and orange from the caviar to give an extra ritzy image to the table. Create a 'set' for a special occasion: choose a geometric damask white cloth and starch it crisply, it will make the perfect backdrop for the strong colours of the tableware, food and drinks. Mesh and metal are essential for the high-tech look, and there are plenty of plates, trays and trolleys to choose from which are not expensive. Arrange white tulips in black lacquer vases and festoon the room with black and white balloons – if you fill them with helium they will stay put on the ceiling. Continue the black and white theme by insisting on black tie for gentlemen guests, elegant little black dresses for the ladies, using spotlights and black and white candles to evoke a dramatic mood. For the drinks, serve Margaritas (see page 101) in salt-frosted black glasses as aperitifs, then smart black bottles of cordon negro – a dry Spanish cava – with the food.

GORGONZOLA PRUNES

'Ready to eat' prunes, sometimes also called 'no need to soak' prunes, are perfect for stuffing as they do not need soaking and therefore retain their shape. They are available at most supermarkets. Large black grapes can be stuffed in the same way as these prunes, and you could use all plain full-fat soft cheese instead of the blue cheese suggested here.

INGREDIENTS

30 'ready to eat' prunes

175 g (6 oz) Gorgonzola cheese, rind removed, at room temperature

175 g (6 oz/¾ cup) full-fat soft cheese (cream cheese)

freshly ground black pepper

100 g (4 oz/1 cup) shelled walnuts, roughly chopped

Cook the prunes in boiling water for 5 minutes to plump them up. Drain and leave until cool enough to handle.

Meanwhile, mash the Gorgonzola in a bowl, then gradually work in the soft cheese. Add pepper to taste.

Cut a slit in each prune and carefully remove the stone (pit). Open out the prunes, taking care not to break them completely in half. Spoon the cheese filling into a piping (pastry) bag fitted with a small star nozzle (tube) and pipe the filling in the centre of each prune. Sprinkle the filling with the nuts.

*V*elvety smooth, unbelievably rich
and creamy, Black Grape
Cheesecake (page 125) is an
exquisite-looking dessert for a stylish soirée. It is very quick to prepare, and can
be made 2–3 days in advance. If you like, you can cover the entire surface of
the cake with grapes, or serve extra grapes separately.

BLINI

Blini, yeasted buckwheat pancakes, are traditionally topped with caviar, however, this is prohibitively expensive for a large number of people, and the black lumpfish roe suggested here will be an acceptable alternative for most guests. If you like, you can also use red lumpfish roe and the orange-coloured 'salmon caviar', both of which will provide a dramatic colour contrast.

INGREDIENTS

225 g (½ lb) buckwheat flour

1 sachet easybake dried yeast

300 ml (½ pint/1¼ cups) tepid milk and water

225 g (8 oz/2 cups) strong plain (unbleached all-purpose) white flour

1 teaspoon salt

2 eggs, separated

50 g (2 oz/½ stick) butter, melted

450 ml (¾ pint/2 cups) milk

TO SERVE

600 ml (1 pint/2½ cups) soured cream

about 900 g (2 lb) lumpfish roe

Put the buckwheat flour in a large bowl, add the yeast and stir well to mix. Stir in the tepid milk and water gradually. Cover the bowl with cling film (plastic wrap) and leave to rise in a warm place for 30 minutes.

Meanwhile, sift the plain flour into a separate bowl with the salt. Make a well in the centre, add the egg yolks and melted butter and beat with a wooden spoon, adding the milk a little at a time and gradually drawing in the flour to make a smooth batter. Beat into the buckwheat dough, cover again and leave to rise for a further 1 hour.

Whisk the egg whites until stiff and fold into the risen batter. Grease a heavy pancake or frying pan (skillet) with a little butter and heat until very hot. Drop dessertspoonfuls of the batter into the pan, spacing them well apart. Cook for 1 minute or until bubbles appear on the surface, then turn over and cook for the same time on the other side. Repeat to make about 100 pancakes altogether, re-greasing the pan as necessary and keeping each batch warm after cooking.

To serve: arrange the blini on trays or large serving platters. Top each one with a heaped teaspoon each of soured cream and lumpfish roe.

BLACK GRAPE
CHEESECAKE

Crush the biscuits finely in a food processor (or in a bowl with the end of a straight rolling pin). Stir in the melted butter. Turn the mixture into a buttered 20 cm (8 inch) springform cake tin and press with the back of a metal spoon to coat the bottom evenly. Chill in the refrigerator for about 30 minutes until firm.

Meanwhile, beat the cheese until soft, then beat in the lemon rind, sugar and eggs until evenly mixed. Turn the mixture into the biscuit-lined tin and level the surface. Bake at 150°C (300°F) mark 2 for 45 minutes until the filling feels firm in the centre. Turn off the oven, but leave the cheesecake in the oven until cold. Chill in the refrigerator overnight.

To serve: remove the cheesecake carefully from the tin and place on a serving plate. Arrange the grape halves around the outer edge.

For 10–15 people you will need to make 2 or 3 of these cheesecakes, according to the appetites of your guests. It is important to use the exact cheese specified for a rich, creamy texture.

INGREDIENTS

175 g (6 oz) digestive biscuits (graham crackers)

100 g (4 oz/1 stick) unsalted butter, melted

700 g (1½ lb) Philadelphia cheese, at room temperature

finely grated rind of 1–2 lemons, according to taste

100 g (4 oz/½ cup) caster (superfine) sugar

2 eggs, beaten

12–15 black grapes, halved and seeded